FREE MONEY

FREE MONEY
For Small Businesses and Entrepreneurs
Revised and Updated

Laurie Blum

WILEY

John Wiley & Sons, Inc.

New York • Chichester • Brisbane • Toronto • Singapore

Library of Congress Cataloging in Publication Data

Blum, Laurie.
    Free money for small businesses and entrepreneurs / Laurie Blum. —
Rev. and updated.
        p.   cm.
    Bibliography: p.
    ISBN 0-471-62337-7. —ISBN 0-471-62338-5 (pbk.)
    1. Small business—United States—Finance—Directories.
2. Commercial loans—United States—Directories. 3. Endowments—
United States—Directories. 4. Federal aid to community
development—United States—Directories. I. Title.
HG4027.7.B58 1989   89-31894
658.15'224—dc20   CIP

Printed in the United States of America

90 10 9 8 7 6 5 4 3 2

To J. T. O'Hara,
who always said it was possible,
and to Stuart D. Wechsler,
who made it possible.

It isn't money that sustains me—it's the faith I have
in myself, in my own powers. In spirit I'm a
millionaire—maybe that's the best thing about
America, that you believe you'll rise again.

—Henry Miller

Contents

Introduction

Are you a small business person frustrated by lack of investment capital or by lenders unwilling to take risks? Are you a would-be entrepreneur with no idea of how you are going to raise the needed capital to start your business? Or do you own a medium-sized business that is looking for expansion capital? Believe it or not, the nonprofit community has billions of dollars available to entrepeneurs and profit-making businesses. The money takes the form of outright grants (which is money that does not have to be paid back), equity investments, letters of credit, and direct loans (often at extremely low interest rates such as four percent and often with extended time periods and flexible terms for repayment).

The information presented in this book demonstrates that there is a large yet often untapped source of alternative venture and expansion capital for both profit and nonprofit organizations. Remember, however, that funding sources are not without restrictions. Do you just walk up, hold out your hand, and expect someone to put money in it? Of course not. It takes time, effort, and thought on your part. You are going to have to find out who is giving away money. You are going to have to fill out applications. You may meet with frustration or rejection somewhere down the road. The odds, however, are in your favor that you will qualify for some sort of funding.

The hardest part has always been finding the sources of money. That is why I wrote this book. I have written books on grant money for students and individuals in the arts, and I have written a previous edition of this book. This new edition of *Free Money* includes updated funding information that I have been using very successfully for my clients. Much of the information in this book has never been made available to the general public.

I wanted to make this book as easy to use as possible. Since I find it tedious to use an index, I have organized the book to eliminate the need for one. The listings are divided into three sections: (1) program-related investments, (2) flow-through funding and, (3) federal money. Within these sections the listings are arranged by geographic location (where you or your business are located) and type of business (real estate, import/export; I deliberately kept these categories broad). Check all three sections to see which grants apply to you.

You'll find all the details you'll need, including the total amount of money that is awarded, the number of grants or loans given, the range of the monies given, and the average size of an award. Note that the use of the word "minority" in this book refers to people who are either black, Hispanic, American Indian, or female.

By the time this book is published, some of the information contained here will have changed. No reference book can be as up to date as the reader (or author) would like. Names, addresses, dollar amounts, telephone numbers, and other data are always in flux; however, most of the information will not have changed. Good luck.

HOW TO APPLY

Applying for nonprofit money takes work, as well as some thought and organization. First comes the sorting-out process. Go through each section of the book and mark all the foundations that could potentially give you money. (Don't be dissuaded from applying if the money given is a low interest loan or if the award is donated technical services.) Pay close attention to the restrictions and eliminate the least likely foundations. You should apply for a number of grants and awards; the same material you put together for one application can be used for most, if not all, of the other applications.) Although none of the foundations in this book requires an application fee, the effort you will have to put in will probably limit you to no more than eight applications (if you are ambitious and want to apply to more than eight foundations, go right ahead). Write or call the most likely foundations to get a copy of their guidelines. In cases where the contact's name is not listed, begin your letter: To Whom It May Concern. If you call, just request the guidelines; do not cross-examine the person who answers the phone.

Grant applications take time to fill out. Often, you will be required to write one or more essays. Be neat! You may very well prepare a top-notch proposal, but it won't look good if it's done in a sloppy manner. Proposals should always be typed and double spaced. Be sure to make a copy of the proposal. I've learned the hard way that there is nothing worse than having the foundation or governmental agency not be able to find your proposal and your having to reconstruct it because you didn't keep a copy. You may be asked for your tax return and other financial records. (Don't worry, you won't be penalized for having money in the bank or having run an effective business.) You may be asked to include personal references. Be sure to get strong references; call each person you plan to list, and ask them if they feel com-

fortable giving you a reference. Remember, you have to
sell yourself and convince the grantors to give money to
you and not to someone else.

The Proposal

A grant proposal will include a concise and tight narrative description of the project or business that you are
attempting to fund. Remember, it is essential that you
sell your project to the potential granter in the very first
paragraph. The following outline should give you a good
idea of how to put together the necessary components of
a good proposal:

1. **Title page:** Name of applicant, organization (nonprofit
   or fiscal sponsor), or business.
2. **First paragraph:** Clear and precise statement of
   purpose. Your statement of purpose should answer
   the following three questions:
   a. What do you hope to accomplish?
   b. How do you plan to accomplish your goals? (What
      activities, programs, or services will you undertake
      to accomplish your goals? Would you characterize
      these efforts as service related, advocacy focused,
      or public education related?)
   c. For whose benefit does your organization or busi-
      ness exist? (Whom does your organization or busi-
      ness currently serve or plan to serve? How specifi-
      cally can you define your prime constituents by age,
      sex, geography, minority group status, or income?)
3. **Body of narrative:** Try to keep this to two or three
   double-spaced paragraphs at the most. Brevity is the
   key! The body of this narrative should include a very
   specific indication of the proposed goals of the project
   and how the objectives will be met.

4. **Attachments:**
   a. For a profit-making business, the following items should be attached to the narrative:
      1. Use of loan (working capital, land etc.)
      2. Balance sheets
      3. Profit and loss statements (for 90 days and three years)
      4. Accounts receivables
      5. Earnings projection (for one year)
      6. Business and personal IRS returns (last three years)
      7. Résumés of management
      8. Any machinery or equipment owned (cost/name of seller)
      9. Any lawsuits or bankruptcies
   b. For nonprofit organizations or profit-making businesses working with a fiscal sponsor the following items should be attached to the narrative:
      1. A copy of the nonprofit organization's 501-C-3 IRS letter that documents tax-exempt status
      2. A board of directors list
      3. A list of past and present funding support (government, corporate, and foundation)
      4. Budgets (Last year, current year, and projected)
      5. One or two good press articles on the organization if available

The following are examples of two excellent proposals—one for a profit-making enterprise and the other for a nonprofit organization.

Sample Proposal: Profit

Contact
Company
Address

Dear

Year after year medical insurance premiums spiral upward and the complexity of filing claims increases. Medicare's budget has become an enormous black hole where money falls in but little or no correlation can be made to the quality of medical care that is received in turn. The American Medical Association (AMA) has come under frequent attack for protecting doctors who have been negligent. The burdens of the system raise the cost of medical care for all Americans, causing us all to suffer the effects and costs.

Medinet is a high-speed information system designed to link medical services and related industries. Medinet could be the cornerstone of a comprehensive evolution of medicine, revolutionizing the medical industry with the same convenience and efficiency that the ATM card brought to the banking industry. Through the application of technilogical advances in networking, data storage/access, transmission, and communications combined with medical expertise, Medinet will vastly improve the delivery, tracking, and availability of medical information, billing, and medical treatment utilization.

Medicine still lags far behind many other fields in the use of computer information systems. To improve its control over itself, its costs, and its vulnerabilities of irregularities in fees and services, Medinet will benefit doctors, patients, insurance companies, and government medical agencies by providing a unified standard network and efficiency of information. There are numerous advantages to this system, since its function is the reliable and timely management and distribution of information. Medinet can serve as a secured archive for medical information. This information may be utilized by insurance companies, government agencies, or universities to typify or track trends in the population. This information can also determine relative concentrations of certain diseases and injuries and establish standards for treatment or cost of medical care. Short- and long-term medical problems can be identified, and adjustments can be made more gradually to ensure rates and premium standards for medical care. Medinet could be used to reduce the number of suits due to wrongful deaths and other forms of negligence by showing that a minimum and a maximum level of competent treatment does exist in the medical industry.

Physically, Medinet is a network of computer systems. Each system consists of building blocks of fast RISC (Reduced Instruction Set Computer) based computers. With this architecture, Medinet can provide several times the performance of the most powerful single computer designs over a distribution link that allows redundancy and high reliability, low purchase and maintenance costs, and geographical flexibility.

Our computer systems will be linked to a high-speed network to provide fast transfer and sharing of data among distant locations. Networks are designed for fast, efficient communications among different hosts and client sites. By using localized networks feeding into larger systems, networks can minimize the amount of redundant hardware and phone costs. At the same time, we can provide flexible systems that adapt themselves to the amount of traffic and work load needed. Medinet will be an efficient data management system that will radically improve the delivery and quality of medical care coverage for the insurance company, the patient, and the provider.

Medicare is by far the most significant potential

Medinet user. Our capacity to collect, verify, and store information in a timely fashion and with greater accuracy will exceed any current technology. Medicare will have access to obtain information on medical costs and treatments. There will be an opportunity to control the rising costs of medical care and observe trends in costs and participation in different programs. Insurance companies will have an opportunity to use similar tracking, resulting in better budget control and in the lowering of overall Medicare spending. Patients, doctors, and Medicare end up suffering together from the lack of uniformity in the quality of medical care, from deep insurance premium hikes, and from spending controls.

Because we feel *(corporation, foundation)* would be interested in the implementation of Medinet, we are now approaching you for a contribution of $_____. Medinet will be the system to bring together the patient, the doctors, and the insurance companies, saving valuable time and lives. It will put the trust back into our health care system and practitioners.

We have also enclosed additional materials about Medinet for your information. If you have any questions or need additional materials about Medinet for your information, please do not hesitate to call me at (213) 462-5292.

Sincerely,

Michael Gitter, M.D.

MG/cm
encl.

Sample Proposal: Nonprofit

Contact
Company
Address

Dear

Without the help of corporate and foundation support here in Los Angeles, there is a chance we will have to close our doors for good in the fall of 1988.

Few organizations in Los Angeles have worked as long and as hard as the Inner City Cultural Center has to bridge the gaps between the diverse cultural and ethnic groups that make up this vast city. Since the Center's founding in 1966, it has been dedicated to providing performing artists with meaningful opportunities to use their talents and abilities to make significant statements about and to the multi-cultural communities of Los Angeles. At the same time, the Center has committed itself to enriching these communities by bringing outstanding works of creative expression, including theatre, dance, music, and poetry, to audiences who otherwise would have little or no access to them.

The communities' response to the artistic excellence offered by the Inner City Cultural Center confirms our belief that the Center does serve a deeply felt need. Attendance at the Center's performances and events has increased steadily over the years and, at present, the Center can boast one of the highest number of sold-out houses of any theatres in Los Angeles.

Productions at the Center have ranged from the Greek classics to the latest in contemporary theatre and dance. The Center has been the site of numerous world premieres, including the first productions of works it has commissioned. All productions are of the highest professional caliber possible within the means of the Center. And the performances—including memorable appearances by the likes of Paul Winfield, Beah Richards, Lawrence Hilton-Jacobs, Carmen Zapata, and the Dance Theatre of Harlem—have consistently received critical praise.

In addition to the full spectrum of productions, the Center also has classes, competitions, and training and intern programs designed to broaden the opportunities of talented young people in the performing arts. The Center can point with pride to the large number of performers who have launched their careers in its classrooms and on its stages. They have learned and practiced all aspects of their craft in the Center's classes and have tested their ability in the Ira Aldridge Annual Acting Competition and the ICCC Short Play Competition.

The Inner City Cultural Center is among this country's very few cultural organizations founded and operated by people of color. As such, the Center has, for the past two decades, been a great source of pride to the black, Hispanic, Asian and white communities. It has demonstrated time and time again the great potential each community has for making a serious, positive contribution to the cultural life of our city and of our country. The Center encourages a true dialogue between the communities, striving for a greater understanding that will improve the quality of life for us all.

Since 1972, the Center has been located in its own building near the corner of Pico and Vermont in a section of Los Angeles that is the home of well-established black, Hispanic, and Asian neighborhoods. With its three theatres, classrooms, rehearsal rooms, and library, the Center is looked on as an important cultural resource by the surrounding communities, and it has received the majority of its support—both earned and contributed—from those who use it the most.

The Inner City Cultural Center today finds its future in serious jeopardy. The building code for the City of

Los Angeles mandates that all large structures within the city limits be able to withstand the force of an earthquake of considerable magnitude. The Center's building is sound and stable (it sustained no damage during October's quake), and it will continue to meet the Center's needs in terms of space. However, if it is not brought up to the City's earthquake standards, the Center will be forced to close its doors.

The Center had been working with local engineers on a gradual renovation that would ease the financial strain such extensive rebuilding would have on the Center by completing the job over a number of years. Unfortunately, the city has recently revealed its new timetable for the project: it must be finished by the fall of next year.

Thus, we are now making this urgent appeal to both corporations and foundations who share our concern for a cultural life that encompasses all the communities in our city. If we do not reach our goal of raising the estimated $200,000 necessary to meet the city's requirements by next fall, it could bring our two-decade record of accomplishments to an end.

We sincerely hope that, in recognizing the importance of our work and the seriousness of our situation, you will contribute $_____ to our Renovation Fund, thereby helping to ensure that the Inner City Cultural Center can continue serving those who have traditionally been underserved here in Los Angeles.

Enclosed please find some additional information about the Inner City Cultural Center. If you should need more information, please do not hesitate to call us.

Sincerely,

Gene Bolande

GB/blp
encl.

PROGRAM-RELATED INVESTMENTS

A program-related investment (PRI) is an investment a foundation makes in a nonprofit organization, a profit-making business, or an individual that furthers the charitable objectives of the foundation (housing for low-income residents or expansion capital for a small manufacturing firm, which in turn will allow for the hiring of more workers). PRIs traditionally take the form of outright grants, equity investments, letters of credit, donated services (which can range from copying equipment to consultants), and direct loans (the loans are usually offered at extremely low interest rates, such as four percent, and often with extended time periods and flexible terms for repayment).

PRIs as they exist today date back only as far as 1968. However, there were a few earlier examples. Benjamin Franklin created a charitable trust in the late eighteenth century to lend money to "young married artificers" at one percentage point below prevailing interest rates to help them in establishing themselves in business. The Russell Sage Foundation invested in innovative garden apartments in the 1920s. However, this instrument of philanthropy, the use of the investing process to carry out a foundation's program purposes, has gone virtually unused for most of America's philanthropic history.

PRIs are invaluable sources of money for established businesses and, particularly, for start-up situations. Commercial investors usually are unable to invest in many socially beneficial projects because the financial return is too low. Foundations, however, will invest in enterprises that many commercial investors would consider too speculative. They will act as patient investors, willing to wait through the difficult and often unprofitable early years of a business' life with the expectation that profitability will come and that the investment (if the PRI takes the form of an equity investment) will pay an acceptable return. If a foundation is willing to provide a portion of the needed financing through a PRI with a below-market rate of return (or no return at all), then the recipient may be able to obtain the remainder of the financing from commercial investors or lenders. The main function of the PRI, however, is to fulfill a major charitable objective.

An example of a program-related investment is the loan made available at 3 percent during a time of double-digit interest rates by the Collins Foundation to rehabilitate the Butte Hotel, a single-room-occupancy hotel (SRO) in downtown Portland, Oregon. The hotel was renovated through the Burnside Consortium, a nonprofit umbrella organization of civic groups, businesses, and individuals set up to improve the quality of life in downtown Portland. The Consortium's first housing project had been the rehabilitation of the Rich Hotel, also an SRO. The Consortium worked with the owner to attract Housing and Urban Development (HUD) neighborhood self-help grants and loans provided by the local urban renewal agency. The Collins Foundation seed grant was of great importance because of the Foundation's willingness to "take a chance" on a project that at the start "had no money, no lease with the owner, and no technical assistance money to do a feasibility study."

PRIs can be made directly to profit-making businesses and individuals, though sometimes a foundation will only fund nonprofit organizations. An individual or business can use an established nonprofit corporation as a "flow-through," utilizing their tax-exempt status and thereby eliminating the need to set up a separate non-profit organization. If possible, it is a good idea to work through a nonprofit organization whose purposes and activities are compatible with your own (i.e., if you are building low-income housing in an inner-city neighborhood, work with a foundation that makes grants for community renewal). The established nonprofit organization is usually given 3 to 7 percent of monies raised as a flow-through fee. For further information, see Section II.

1

Program-Related Investments by State

CALIFORNIA

American Honda Foundation
P.O. Box 2205
Torrance, California 90509-2205
(213) 781-4090

Restrictions: Grants for scholarship funds, fellowships, special projects, operating budgets, continuing support, research, building funds, equipment, seed money, annual campaigns, professorships, internships, matching funds, capital campaigns, conferences and seminars, exchange programs, and program-related investments.

$ Given: $613,418 for 16 grants: high $71,854; low $2,500; average $25,000–$50,000.

Assets: $10,040,895

Publications: Grants list, newsletter, informational brochure (including application guidelines), program policy statement, and application guidelines.

Contact: Kathryn A. Carey, Manager
   Application information: application form required

Initial approach: letter or telephone

Copies of proposal: 1

Deadlines: November 1, February 1, May 1, and August 1

Board meeting dates: January, April, July, and October

Final notification: 2 months

The Corcoran Community Foundation
P. O. Box 655
Corcoran, California 93212
(209) 992-5551

Restrictions: Broad purposes: to support organizations benefiting the inhabitants of Corcoran and its surrounding area. Grants awarded for operating budgets, continuing support, seed money, emergency funds, building funds, equipment, land acquisition, matching funds, consulting services, technical assistance, program-related investments, loans, special projects, publications, conferences, and seminars.

$ Given: $104,000 for 26 grants: high $32,500; low $233. Also $12,000 for two loans.

Assets: $1,023,453

Contact: Mike Graville, Executive Director

Initial approach: letter

Copies of proposal: 1

Deadlines: submit proposal preferably in the month preceding board meetings

Board meeting dates: October, December, February, April, June, and August

Final notification: after board meeting

Wallace Alexander Gerbode Foundation
470 Columbus Avenue, Suite 209
San Francisco, California 94133
(415) 391-0911

Restrictions: Support for innovative positive programs and projects with a direct impact on residents of the five San Francisco Bay Area counties or Hawaii.

Focus of giving: Giving limited to programs directly affecting residents of Alameda, Contra Costa, Marin, San Francisco, and San Mateo counties in California and residents of Hawaii.

$ Given: $994,529 for 96 grants: high $60,000; low $300.

Contact: Thomas C. Layton, Executive Director
    Initial approach: letter
    Copies of proposal: 1
    Deadlines: none
    Board meeting dates: 6 times a year
    Final notification: 2 to 3 months

The Luke B. Hancock Foundation
360 Bryant Street
Palo Alto, California 94301
(414) 321-5536

Restrictions: Broad purposes: local giving primarily for job training and employment for youth. Special project grants for consortia with other foundations in areas where there is unmet need; some support for technical assistance and emergency funding.

Focus of giving: Giving limited to California, particularly the five counties of the San Francisco Bay Area.

$ Given: $828,728 for grants.

Contact: Joan H. Wylie, Executive Director
   Initial approach: letter
   Copies of proposal: 1
   Deadlines: none
   Board meeting dates: January, March, June, and September
   Final notification: 3 to 4 months

The Parker Foundation
1200 Prospect Street, Suite 575
La Jolla, California 92037
(619) 456-3038

Restrictions: Giving largely in the form of partial seed money and matching or challenge grants; generally no support that would make an organization dependent on the foundation.

Focus of giving: Giving limited to San Diego County, California.

$ Given: $421,834 for 43 grants: high $55,000; low $100; average $2,000–$20,000.

Publications: Annual report, program policy statement, and application guidelines.

Contact: Judy DiBenedetto, Assistant Secretary
>   **Initial approach:** letter
>   **Copies of proposal:** 6
>   **Deadlines:** none
>   **Board meeting dates:** monthly
>   **Final notification:** 2 months

The San Francisco Foundation
685 Market Street, Suite 910
San Francisco, California 94105
(415) 543-0223

Restrictions: Grants awarded for operating budgets, seed money, building funds, equipment, land acquisition, program-related investments, special projects, loans, and technical assistance.

Focus of giving: Giving limited to the Bay Area, counties of Alameda, Contra Costa, Marin, San Francisco, and San Mateo.

$ Given: $37,753,057 for 683 grants: high $1,000,000; low $100; average $5,000–$75,000. Also $4,307,903 for five loans.

Assets: $461,040,287

Contact: Martin A. Paley, Director
>   **Application information:** application form required
>   **Initial approach:** letter
>   **Copies of proposal:** 1
>   **Deadlines:** none

Board meeting dates: monthly except August; applications are reviewed 6 times each year

Final notification: 3 to 4 months

COLORADO

Coors (Adolph) Foundation
350-C Clayton Street
Denver, Colorado 80206
(303) 388-1636

Restrictions: Grants given for building funds, general purposes, seed money, and program-related investments.

Focus of giving: Giving primarily in Colorado.

$ Given: $4,425,146, including $3,265,690 for grants.

Contact: Linda S. Tafoya, Executive Director
    Initial approach: letter
    Copies of proposal: 1
    Deadlines: 6 weeks prior to meetings
    Board meeting dates: February, May, August, and November
    Final notification: 3 months

Gates Foundation
3200 Cherry Creek South Drive, Suite 630
Denver, Colorado 80209-3247
(303) 722-1881

Restrictions: Grants for continuing support, building funds, capital campaigns, endowment funds, matching funds, program-related investments, renovation projects, seed money, special projects, equipment, fellowships, general purposes, land acquisition, publications, and technical assistance.

Focus of giving: Giving limited to Colorado, especially the Denver area, except for foundation-initiated grants.

$ Given: $3,367,020 for 106 grants: high $850,000; average $5,000–$100,000.

Assets: $84,600,000

Publications: Annual report, informational brochure (including application guidelines), program policy statement, and grants list.

Contact: F. Charles Froelicher, Executive Director

   Initial approach: telephone

   Copies of proposal: 1

   Deadlines: February 1, April 15, August 1, and October 15

   Board meeting dates: April 1, June 15, October 1, and December 15

   Final notification: 2 weeks following meetings

The Piton Foundation
511 16th Street, Suite 700
Denver, Colorado 80202
(303) 825-6246

Restrictions: To encourage personal effort toward self-realization, to promote the development of strong cooperative relationships between the public and private sectors with emphasis on local involvement, and to improve conditions and opportunities for persons inadequately served by the institutions of society. Support for individual volunteer agencies to encourage improved management and service effectiveness; some giving also for civic, conservation, and health programs.

Grants awarded for operating budgets, seed money, emergency funds, consulting services, technical assistance, and program-related investments.

Focus of giving: Giving primarily in Colorado, with emphasis on the Denver metropolitan area, especially for community economic development and low-income, affordable housing. No grants for basic research, long-range support, debt reduction, building or endowment funds, media projects, or matching gifts.

$ Given: $5,660,983 for grants: high $350,000. Also $79,992 for 54 grants to individuals.

Contact: Phyllis Buehele, Grants Administrator
 Initial approach: letter
 Copies of proposal: 1
 Deadlines: none
 Board meeting dates: as required
 Final notification: approximately 4 months

Lowe Foundation
Colorado Judicial Center
Two East 14th Avenue
Denver, Colorado 80203
(303) 837-3750

Restrictions: Grants for building funds, equipment, general purposes, operating budgets, program-related investments, and seed money.

Focus of giving: Giving primarily in Colorado.

$ Given: $115,000 for 21 grants: high $15,000; low $1,500; average $6,000.

Assets: $2,395,000

Publications: 990-PF, and application guidelines.

Contact: Luis D. Rovira, President
> **Initial approach:** letter
> **Copies of proposal:** 5
> **Deadlines:** submit proposal preferably in January; deadline February 28
> **Board meeting dates:** March and November

Fishback (Harmes C.) Foundation Trust
Eight Village Road
Englewood, Colorado 80110
(303) 789-1753

Restrictions: Grants for capital campaigns, continuing support, endowment funds, program-related investments, and scholarship funds.

Focus of giving: Giving primarily in Denver, Colorado.

$ Given: $76,300 for 34 grants: high $20,000; low $250.

Assets: $1,739,249

Contact: Katharine H. Stapleton, Trustee
> **Initial approach:** letter
> **Copies of proposal:** 1
> **Deadlines:** none
> **Board meeting dates:** quarterly

CONNECTICUT

Connecticut Mutual Life Foundation
140 Garden Street
Hartford, Connecticut 06154
(203) 727-6500

Restrictions: Largely for education, low- and moderate-income housing, and social purposes. Grants given for operating budgets, continuing support, seed money, building funds, matching funds, consulting services, technical assistance, program-related investments, special projects, conferences, and seminars.

Focus of giving: Giving primarily in the Hartford, Connecticut area.

$ Given: $769,691 for 102 grants: average $3,000–$6,000.

Assets: $8,043,787

Contact: Astrida R. Olds, Assistant Vice President
    Initial approach: letter, full proposal, or telephone
    Copies of proposal: 1
    Deadlines: none
    Board meeting dates: March and November ˉ
    Final notification: 3 months

Primerica Foundation
American Lane
P.O. Box 3610
Greenwich, Connecticut 06830-3610
(203) 552-2148

Restrictions: Grants for operating budgets, seed money, emergency funds, employee matching gifts, scholarships, fellowships, special projects, continuing support, and program-related investments.

Focus of giving: Giving primarily to national organizations, with some emphasis on areas of company operations. Generally no grants for capital drives.

$ Given: $3,532,943 for grants: high $250,000; low $100; average $50,000. Also $167,941 for employee matching gifts.

Publications: Annual report, program policy statement, and application guidelines.

Contact: Peter Goldberg, Vice President
   Initial approach: letter or proposal
   Copies of proposal: 1
   Deadlines: none
   Board meeting dates: every 8 to 10 weeks
   Final notification: 2 months

DELAWARE

Crystal Trust
1088 DuPont Building
Wilmington, Delaware 19898
(302) 774-8421

Restrictions: Grants awarded for seed money, building funds, equipment, land acquisition, and program-related investments.

Focus of giving: Giving primarily in Delaware.

$ Given: $843,260 for 46 grants: high $100,000; low $2,000; average $10,000–$20,000.

Contact: Burt C. Pratt, Director
  Initial approach: letter
  Copies of proposal: 1
  Deadline: October 1
  Board meeting date: November
  Final notification: December 31

Raskob Foundation for Catholic Activities, Inc.
P.O. Box 4019
Wilmington, Delaware 19807
(302) 655-4440

Restrictions: Grants for operating budgets, seed money, emergency funds, equipment, land acquisition, matching funds, conferences and seminars, program-related investments, renovation projects, and special projects.

$ Given: $2,879,026 for grants.

Publications: Biennial report (including application guidelines) and application guidelines.

Contact: Gerard S. Garey, President
  Application information: application form required
  Initial approach: letter
  Copies of proposal: 1
  Deadlines: applications accepted for spring meeting from December 15 to February 15; applications accepted for fall meeting from June 15 to August 15
  Board meeting dates: spring and fall
  Final notification: 6 months

DISTRICT OF COLUMBIA

The Hitachi Foundation
1509 22nd Street N.W.
Washington, D.C. 20037
(202) 457-0588

Restrictions: Grants for general purposes, operating budgets, program-related investments, seed money, special projects, and technical assistance.

$ Given: $525,323 for 24 grants: high $118,400; low $1,000; average $35,000. Also $15,000 for loans.

Publications: Annual report (including application guidelines), program policy statement, application guidelines, and newsletter.

Contact: Felicia B. Lynch, Vice President, Programs

Initial approach: letter of no more than three pages; if project is of interest, a more detailed proposal will be invited

Copies of proposal: 1

Deadlines: February 1, June 1, and October 1

Board meeting dates: February, June, and October to review preliminary requests

Final notification: 4 weeks

The Community Foundation of Greater
Washington, Inc.
1002 Wisconsin Avenue N.W.
Washington, D.C. 20007
(202) 338-8993

Restrictions: Grants for seed money, emergency funds, technical assistance, program-related investments, loans, special projects, research, publications, conferences, and seminars.

$ Given: $1,915,918 for 200 grants: high $140,850; low $100; average $1,000–$10,000. Also $1,173,457 for six foundation-administered programs and $62,000 for loans.

Publications: Annual report (including application guidelines), informational brochure, and application guidelines.

Contact: Joan Bridges, Director, Washington Clearinghouse Project

    Initial approach: letter

    Copies of proposal: 1

    Deadlines: May and October

    Board meeting dates: March, June, and November

    Final notification: up to 6 months

FLORIDA

Edyth Bush Charitable Foundation, Inc.*
199 East Welbourne Avenue
P. O. Box 1967
Winter Park, Florida 32790-1967
(407) 647-4322

Restrictions: Support for charitable, educational, and health service organizations, with emphasis on human

*Originally incorporated in 1966 in Minnesota; reincorporated in 1973 in Florida.

services, health, higher education, the elderly, and youth. Provides limited number of program-related investment loans for construction, land purchase, emergency, or similar purposes to organizations otherwise qualified to receive grants.

Focus of giving: Primarily local giving within 100 miles of Winter Park.

$ Given: $2,254,585 for 68 grants: high $200,000; low $1,000; average $15,000–$50,000. Also $106,921 for four foundation-administered programs.

Assets: $40,287,978

Publications: 990-PF, program policy statement, and application guidelines.

Donor: Edyth Bush

Contact: H. Clifford Lee, President
  Initial approach: telephone or full proposal
  Copies of proposal: 2
  Deadlines: September 1 or January 1; May 30 if funds are available
  Board meeting dates: usually in October, March, July, and as required
  Final notification: 3 months after board meeting

The Wilder Foundation
P. O. Box 99
Key Biscayne, Florida 33149

Restrictions: Support for general purposes, building funds, endowment funds, research, scholarship funds, and matching funds.

Focus of giving: Giving primarily in Florida.

$ Given: $126,956 for 18 grants: high $55,000; low $80.

Assets: $962,796

Contact: Rita or Gary Wilder, President and Vice President

> **Initial approach:** proposal
> **Copies of proposal:** 1
> **Deadline:** submit proposal before September
> **Board meeting dates:** monthly

GEORGIA

Metropolitan Atlanta Community Foundation, Inc.
The Hurt Building, Suite 449
Atlanta, Georgia 30303
(404) 688-5525

Restrictions: Grants for seed money, emergency funds, building funds, equipment, land acquisition, technical assistance, program-related investments, special projects, publications, capital campaigns, matching funds, and renovation projects.

$ Given: $10,223,081 for grants: high $1,000,000; low $50; average $3,000–$5,000.

Publications: Annual report, program policy statement, and application guidelines.

Contact: Alicia Philipp, Executive Director

Application information: application form required

Initial approach: letter or telephone

Copies of proposal: 1

Deadlines: June 1, September 1, December 1, and March 1

Board meeting dates: July, October, January, and April

Final notification: 6 weeks

The Coca-Cola Foundation
One Coca-Cola Plaza
Atlanta, Georgia 30313
(404) 676-3740

Restrictions: Grants for annual campaigns, scholarship funds, continuing support, operating budgets, program-related investments, and special projects.

$ Given: $3,666,464 for 149 grants: high $371,031; low $200; and $500,000 for loans.

Assets: $8,772,658

Publications: Annual report, application guidelines, and informational brochure (including application guidelines).

Contact: Margaret J. Cox, Executive Director

Initial approach: proposal

Board meeting dates: February, May, July, and November

Final notification: 90 to 120 days

HAWAII

Wallace Alexander Gerbode Foundation
470 Columbus Avenue, Suite 209
San Francisco, California 94133
(415) 391-0911

Restrictions: Support for innovative positive programs and projects with a direct impact on residents of the five San Francisco Bay Area counties or Hawaii.

Focus of giving: Giving limited to programs directly affecting residents of Alameda, Contra Costa, Marin, San Francisco, and San Mateo counties in California and residents of Hawaii.

$ Given: $994,529 for 96 grants: high $60,000; low $300.

Contact: Thomas C. Layton, Executive Director
    Initial approach: letter
    Copies of proposal: 1
    Deadlines: none
    Board meeting dates: 6 times a year
    Final notification: 2 to 3 months

IDAHO

Northwest Area Foundation
West 975 First National Bank Building
St. Paul, Minnesota 55101
(612) 224-9635

Restrictions: Grants generally for experimental and demonstration projects that promise significant impact on the community and the well-being of society but for which there is not now general support.

Focus of giving: Giving limited to an eight-state region that includes Idaho, Iowa, Minnesota, Montana, North Dakota, Oregon, South Dakota, and Washington.

$ Given: $6,967,105 for 196 grants: high $250,000; low $150; average $20,000–$60,000.

Contact: Terry Tinson, President

    Initial approach: telephone, letter, or proposal

    Copies of proposal: 2

    Deadlines: varies

    Board meeting dates: bimonthly, beginning in February

    Final notification: 60 to 90 days

ILLINOIS

The Field Foundation of Illinois, Inc.
135 South LaSalle Street
Chicago, Illinois 60603
(312) 263-3211

Restrictions: Health, welfare, education, cultural activities and civic affairs. Grants focused on youth agencies, race relations, and the aged. Support for building funds, emergency funds, equipment, special projects, and land acquisition.

Focus of giving: Giving primarily in the Chicago, Illinois area.

$ Given: $1,475,357 for 69 grants: high $60,000; low $1,000; average $10,000–$20,000.

Assets: $22,926,924

Contact: Lorraine Madsen, President
   Initial approach: full proposal
   Board meeting dates: quarterly

The Meyer-Ceco Foundation
c/o The Ceco Corporation
One Tower Lane, Suite 2300
Oak Brook Terrace, Illinois 60181
(312) 242-2000

Restrictions: Continuing support and program-related investments.

Focus of giving: Giving primarily in Illinois.

$ Given: $252,915 for 140 grants: high $32,000; low $100; average $500–$1,500.

Assets: $3,878,715

Publications: 990-PF.

Contact: R. J. Stankus, Assistant Treasurer, Taxes

INDIANA

Cummins Engine Foundation
Box Number 3005
Columbus, Indiana 47202-3005
(812) 377-3569

Restrictions: Primarily on local community needs, youth, civil rights; grants also for national needs that combine equal opportunity and excellence.

Focus of giving: Giving primarily in areas of company operations, particularly the Columbus, Indiana area.

$ Given: $1,711,063 for 120 grants: high $272,296; low $500; average $2,500–$15,000.

Contact: Adele Vincent, Executive Director

    Initial approach: full proposal or letter

    Copies of proposal: 1

    Deadlines: none

    Board meeting dates: February, July, September, and December

    Final notification: 1 to 3 months

Heritage Fund of Bartholomew County, Inc.
P.O. Box 1547
Columbus, Indiana 47202
(812) 376-7772

Restrictions: Grants given for operating budgets, continuing support, seed money, emergency funds, deficit financing, building funds, equipment, land acquisition, matching funds, consulting services, technical assistance, program-related investments, special projects, conferences, and seminars.

Focus of giving: Giving primarily in Bartholomew County, Indiana.

$ Given: $9,938 for four grants.

Contact: Edward F. Sullivan, Executive Director

Olive B. Cole Foundation, Inc.
Cole Capital Corporation
3242 Mallard Cove Lane
Fort Wayne, Indiana 46804
(219) 436-2182

Restrictions: Grants given for seed money, building funds, equipment, land acquisition, matching funds, program-related investments, general purposes, and continuing support.

Focus of giving: Giving limited to the LaGrange, Steuben, and Noble counties.

$ Given: $337,462 for 28 grants: high $70,000; low $1,000; average $12,052. Also $118,018 for grants to individuals.

Contact: John E. Hogan, Jr., Executive Vice President

  Application information: application form required

  Initial approach: letter

  Copies of proposal: 7

  Deadlines: none

  Board meeting dates: February, May, August, and November

  Final notification: 4 months

IOWA

Northwest Area Foundation
West 975 First National Bank Building
St. Paul, Minnesota 55101
(612) 224-9635

Restrictions: Grants generally for experimental and demonstration projects that promise significant impact on the community and the well-being of society but for which there is not now general support.

Focus of giving: Giving limited to an eight-state region that includes Idaho, Iowa, Minnesota, Montana, North Dakota, Oregon, South Dakota, and Washington.

$ Given: $6,967,105 for 196 grants: high $250,000; low $150; average $20,000–$60,000.

Contact: Terry Tinson, President

    Initial approach: telephone, letter, or proposal

    Copies of proposal: 2

    Deadlines: varies

    Board meeting dates: bimonthly, beginning in February

    Final notification: 60 to 90 days

KANSAS

The Powell Family Foundation
10990 Roe Avenue
P.O. Box 7270
Shawnee Mission, Kansas 66207
(913) 345-3000

Restrictions: Grants given for operating budgets, seed money, emergency funds, equipment, program-related investments, conferences and seminars, matching funds, and general purposes.

Focus of giving: Giving limited to Kansas City, Kansas and the surrounding community.

$ Given: $1,191,538 for 119 grants: high $147,000; low $200.

Assets: $44,354,020

Contact: Marjorie P. Allen, President
   Initial approach: letter
   Copies of proposal: 2
   Deadlines: 30 days preceding board meetings
   Board meeting dates: usually in January, April, July, and October
   Final notification: 60 days

LOUISIANA

The Lupin Foundation
3715 Prytania Street, Suite 403
New Orleans, Louisiana 70115
(504) 897-6125

Restrictions: Grants for equipment, research, scholarship funds, special projects, matching funds, continuing support, general purposes, program-related investments, renovation projects, and seed money.

Focus of giving: Giving primarily in Louisiana. No grants to individuals; no loans.

$ Given: $1,222,469, including $774,650 for 52 grants: high $75,000; low $800; average $15,000.

Assets: $19,482,186

Publications: Application guidelines.
   Application information: application form required
   Initial approach: brief proposal
   Copies of proposal: 9
   Deadlines: none
   Board meeting dates: monthly
   Final notification: 4 to 6 weeks

MASSACHUSETTS

Godfrey M. Hyams Trust
One Boston Place, 33rd Floor
Boston, Massachusetts 02108
(617) 720-2238

Restrictions: Emphasis on youth agencies and neighborhood centers; support also for other social service and community development purposes. Grants given for operating budgets, continuing support, annual campaigns, seed money, building funds, equipment, land acquisition, and matching funds.

Focus of giving: Giving limited to the Boston, Massachusetts metropolitan area.

$ Given: $2,793,499, including $2,481,387 for 170 grants: high $87,000; low $2,500; average $5,000–$20,000.

Assets: $36,856,565

Contact: Joan M. Diver, Executive Director

Initial approach: full proposal

Copies of proposal: 6

Deadlines: submit proposal preferably in fall or winter; no set deadline

Board meeting dates: 5 to 6 times a year regularly from October through June

Final notification: 2 to 6 months

The Nathaniel and Elizabeth P. Stevens Foundation
P.O. Box 111
North Andover, Massachusetts 01845
(508) 688-7211

Restrictions: Grants given for general purposes, seed money, emergency funds, building funds, equipment, land acquisition, special projects, matching funds, and program-related investments.

Focus of giving: Giving limited to Massachusetts, with emphasis on the greater Lawrence area.

$ Given: $343,620 for 47 grants: high $50,000; low $750; average $2,000–$5,000.

Assets: $5,527,448

Contact: Elizabeth A. Beland

    Initial approach: full proposal

    Copies of proposal: 1

    Deadlines: none

    Board meeting dates: monthly, except in July and August

    Final notification: 2 months

MICHIGAN

Ann Arbor Area Foundation
121 West Washington, Suite 400
Ann Arbor, Michigan 48104
(313) 663-0401

Restrictions: Support for innovative programs and projects in charitable, religious, scientific, civic, moral, literary, cultural, social, and economic areas. Grants for seed money, emergency funds, building funds, equipment, matching funds, program-related investments, research, special projects, publications, conferences, and seminars.

Focus of giving: Giving limited to the Ann Arbor, Michigan area.

$ Given: $71,022 for 21 grants.

Assets: $1,993,994

Contact: Terry Foster, Executive Director
    Application information: application form required
    Initial approach: telephone
    Deadlines: middle of month prior to meetings
    Board meeting dates: January, March, May, September, and November
    Final notification: 30 to 60 days

Hudson-Webber Foundation
333 West Fort Street
Detroit, Michigan 48226
(313) 963-8991

Restrictions: Concentrates efforts and resources in support of physical revitalization of downtown Detroit, reduction of crime in Detroit, and economic development of southeastern Michigan, with emphasis on the creation of additional employment opportunities.

Focus of giving: Giving primarily in the Wayne, Oakland, and Macomb tricounty area of southeastern Michigan, particularly Detroit.

$ Given: $2,176,592 for 62 grants: high $213,000; low $2,400; average $10,000–$30,000. Also $188,871 for 236 grants to individuals and $43,946 for 11 employee matching gifts.

Contact: Gilbert Hudson, President
     Deadlines: April 15, August 15, and December 15

Albert L. and Louise B. Miller Foundation, Inc.
155 West Van Buren Street
Battle Creek, Michigan 49016
(616) 964-7161

Restrictions: Local municipal improvement, grants for seed money, building funds, equipment, land acquisition, endowment funds, and loans.

Focus of giving: Giving primarily in the Battle Creek, Michigan area.

$ Given: $100,600 for 32 grants, high $18,000; low $400; average $3,000.

Assets: $5,791,706

Contact: Robert B. Miller, Chairman
   Application information: application form required
   Initial approach: letter
   Copies of proposal: 10
   Deadlines: none
   Board meeting dates: monthly
   Final notification: 2 months

MINNESOTA

Charles K. Blandin Foundation*
100 Pokegama Avenue North
Grand Rapids, Minnesota 55744
(218) 326-0523

Restrictions: Local giving for community projects and economic development. Support for seed money, emergency funds, loans, program-related investments, special projects, consulting services, and technical assistance.

Focus of giving: Giving limited to Minnesota, with emphasis on rural Minnesota.

$ Given: $4,192,734 for 152 grants: high $450,000; low $500. Also $215,071 for 378 grants to individuals and $110,000 for two loans.

Assets: $17,651,437

Publications: Annual report, application guidelines, and program policy statement.

*Incorporated in 1941 in Minnesota.

Contact: Paul M. Olson, Executive Director

   Initial approach: letter

   Copies of proposal: 1

   Deadlines: submit proposal preferably 2 months prior to board meetings: March 1, June 1, September 1, and December 1

   Board meeting dates: first week of February, May, August, and November

   Final notification: 2 weeks after board meeting

Mary Andersen Hulings Foundation
c/o Baywood Corporation
287 Central Avenue
Bayport, Minnesota 55003
(612) 439-1557

Restrictions: Support for general purposes, operating budgets, seed money, building funds, program-related investments, and research.

Focus of giving: Giving primarily in Minnesota, with emphasis on Bayport.

$ Given: $191,665 for 62 grants: high $35,000; low $100.

Assets: $4,169,468

Contact: Peggy Scott, Grants Consultant

   Application information: application form required

   Initial approach: letter or proposal

Copies of proposal: 2

Deadlines: submit proposal preferably in March, June, September, or December; no set deadlines

Board meeting dates: May, August, November, and February

Final notification: 3 months

The McKnight Foundation
410 Peavey Building
Minneapolis, Minnesota 55402
(612) 333-4220

Restrictions: Emphasis on grant making in the areas of human and social services in the seven-county Twin Cities metropolitan area and in Minnesota. Multiyear comprehensive programs in mental health and developmental disabilities. Also support for programs for the chronically mentally ill in four different communities. Grants for operating budgets, building funds, seed money, emergency funds, equipment, matching funds, program-related investments, and continuing support.

$ Given: $11,945,119 for 200 grants: high $700,000, low $250, average $5,000–$500,000. Also, $3,519,338 for 53 grants to individuals.

Assets: $509,422,638

Contact: Russell V. Ewald, Executive Vice President

    Initial approach: letter

    Copies of proposal: 7

    Deadlines: March 1, June 1, September 1, and December 1

Board meeting dates: February, May, August, and November

Final notification: 2 1/2 months

The McNeely Foundation
444 Pine Street
St. Paul, Minnesota 55101
(612) 228-4444

Restrictions: Grants for community funds including operating budgets, continuing support, annual campaigns, seed money, emergency funds, building funds, endowment funds, and program-related investments.

Focus of giving: Giving primarily in the St. Paul–Minneapolis, Minnesota area.

$ Given: $120,000 for 20 grants: high $40,000; low $500; average $3,000–$5,000.

Assets: $2,600,000

Contact: Malcolm W. McDonald

    Initial approach: letter

    Copies of proposal: 1

    Deadlines: submit proposal preferably in September or December

    Board meeting dates: March, June, September, and December

North Star Research Foundation
805 Builders Exchange
Minneapolis, Minnesota 55402
(612) 339-8101

Restrictions: Grants for the support of scientific research leading to new technology or new businesses to produce or retain jobs to strengthen the region; also loans to businesses or individuals in the form of program-related investments.

Focus of giving: Giving limited to Minnesota and surrounding states.

$ Given: $50,000 for two foundation-administered programs and $22,000 for two loans.

Assets: $1,462,000

Contact: Henry Doerr, Consultant
  Initial approach: telephone or letter
  Deadlines: none
  Board meeting dates: January, April, July, and October
  Final notification: 120 days

Northwest Area Foundation
West 975 First National Bank Building
St. Paul, Minnesota 55101
(612) 224-9635

Restrictions: Grants generally for experimental and demonstration projects that promise significant impact on the community and the well-being of society but for which there is not now general support.

Focus of giving: Giving limited to an eight-state region that includes Idaho, Iowa, Minnesota, Montana, North Dakota, Oregon, South Dakota, and Washington.

$ Given: $6,967,105 for 196 grants: high $250,000; low $150; average $20,000–$60,000.

Contact: Terry Tinson, President

    Initial approach: telephone, letter, or proposal

    Copies of proposal: 2

    Deadlines: varies

    Board meeting dates: bimonthly, beginning in February

    Final notification: 60 to 90 days

The Saint Paul Foundation
1120 Norwest Center
St. Paul, Minnesota 55101
(612) 224-5463

Restrictions: Support for educational, charitable, cultural, or benevolent purposes of a public nature as well as promotion of the well-being of mankind and, preferably, the inhabitants of St. Paul and its vicinity. Grants for seed money, emergency funds, building funds, equipment, matching funds, special projects, and program-related investments.

$ Given: $13,033,824 for 381 grants: high $9,967,964; low $60. Also $324,168 for seven loans.

Assets: $73,859,367

Contact: Paul A. Verret, President

    Initial approach: telephone, letter, or full proposal

    Copies of proposal: 1

    Deadlines: 3 months before next board meeting

Board meeting dates: Generally in March, June, September, November, and December

MISSISSIPPI

Phil Hardin Foundation
P.O. Box 4329
Meridian, Mississippi 39301
(601) 483-4282

Restrictions: Grants for operating budgets, continuing support, seed money, building funds, equipment, endowment funds, matching funds, program-related investments, special projects, research, publications, conferences, and seminars.

Focus of giving: Giving primarily in Mississippi, but also to out-of-state organizations or programs of benefit to the people of Mississippi.

$ Given: $342,664 for 28 grants: high $150,000; low $500; average $12,000.

Assets: $12,912,048

Contact: C. Thompson Wacaster, Vice President
   Initial approach: telephone, letter, or proposal
   Copies of proposal: 2
   Deadlines: none
   Board meeting dates: as required, usually at least every 2 months

MISSOURI

The H&R Block Foundation
4410 Main Street
Kansas City, Missouri 64111
(816) 932-8424

Restrictions: Support for general purposes, building funds, equipment, land acquisition, matching funds, program-related investments, operating budgets, seed money, emergency funds, and deficit financing.

Focus of giving: Giving limited to the 50-mile area around Kansas City.

$ Given: $233,955 for 131 grants: high $26,000; low $50; average $500–25,000. Also $60,000 for 30 grants to individuals and $5,100 for 22 employee matching gifts.

Assets: $3,739,311

Publications: Informational brochure, program policy statement, and application guidelines.

Donor: H&R Block, Inc.

Contact: Terrance R. Wood, President
 Initial approach: full proposal
 Copies of proposal: 1
 Deadlines: 45 days prior to meetings
 Board meeting dates: March, June, September, and December
 Final notification: 2 weeks after board meeting

Hall Family Foundations
Charitable & Crown Investment—323
P.O. Box 419580
Kansas City, Missouri 64141-6580
(816) 274-5615

Restrictions: Broad purposes, within four main areas of interest: (1) youth, especially education and programs that promote social welfare, health, and character building of young people; (2) economic development; (3) the performing and visual arts; and (4) the elderly.

Focus of giving: Giving limited to the Kansas City, Missouri area.

$ Given: $155,550 for 110 grants to individuals and $3,768,407 for 52 grants: high $1,966,921; low $1,000; average $35,000. Also $130,600 for 89 loans.

Assets: $117,877,180

Contact: Sarah V. Hutchison, Margaret H. Pence, or Wendy Hockaday, Program Officers

    Initial approach: letter

    Copies of proposal: 1

    Deadlines: 4 weeks before board meetings

    Board meeting dates: March, June, September, and December

    Final notification: 4 to 6 weeks

MONTANA

Northwest Area Foundation
West 975 First National Bank Building
St. Paul, Minnesota 55101
(612) 224-9635

Restrictions: Grants generally for experimental and demonstration projects that promise significant impact on the community and the well-being of society but for which there is not now general support.

Focus of giving: Giving limited to an eight-state region that includes Idaho, Iowa, Minnesota, Montana, North Dakota, Oregon, South Dakota, and Washington.

$ Given: $6,967,105 for 196 grants: high $250,000; low $150; average $20,000–$60,000.

Contact: Terry Tinson, President

    Initial approach: telephone, letter, or proposal

    Copies of proposal: 2

    Deadlines: varies

    Board meeting dates: bimonthly, beginning in February

    Final notification: 60 to 90 days

NEW JERSEY

Geraldine R. Dodge Foundation, Inc.
95 Madison Avenue
P.O. Box 1239
Morristown, New Jersey 07960-1239
(201) 540-8442

Restrictions: Grant-making emphasis in New Jersey for projects in population, environment, energy, and other critical areas; programs in the public interest, including development of volunteerism, communications, and study of public issues. Commitment to animal welfare concentrates on national strategies for coping with problems posed by burgeoning populations of pets and stray dogs and cats. Interest in the development of a gentler ethic and reduced societal and domestic violence. Grants for seed money, conferences and seminars, matching funds, general purposes, special projects, publications, and continuing support. No grants to individuals.

$ Given: $4,015,288 for 199 grants: high $285,500; average $5,000–$100,000.

Assets: $97,285,629

Contact: Scott McVay, Executive Director

    Initial approach: letter or full proposal

    Copies of proposal: 1

    Deadlines: submit proposal preferably in March, June, September, or December; deadlines January 1 for animal welfare and local projects, October 1 for critical issues/public interest.

    Board meeting dates: March, June, September, and December

    Final notification: by the end of the month in which board meetings are held

NEW HAMPSHIRE

Norwin S. and Elizabeth N. Bean Foundation*
c/o New Hampshire Charitable Fund
1 South Street
P.O. Box 1335
Concord, New Hampshire 03302-1335
(603) 225-6641

Restrictions: Grants for general purposes, seed money, emergency funds, building funds, equipment, land acquisition, special projects, conferences and seminars, matching funds, loans, program-related investments, and consulting services.

Focus of giving: Giving limited to Amherst and Manchester, New Hampshire.

$ Given: $274,691 for 31 grants: high $75,000; low $350; average $500–$5,000. Also $12,000 for one loan.

Assets: $5,298,067

Publications: Program policy statement and application guidelines.

Donors: Norwin S. Bean, Elizabeth N. Bean

Contact: Deborah Cowan, Associate Director
  Initial approach: letter or telephone
  Copies of proposal: 6

*Trust established in 1957 in New Hampshire; later became an affiliated trust of the New Hampshire Charitable Fund.

Deadlines: February 15, May 15, August 15, and November 15

Board meeting dates: March, June, September, and December

NEW MEXICO

Carlsbad Foundation, Inc.*
116 South Canyon
Carlsbad, New Mexico 88220
(505) 887-1131

Restrictions: Support given in the form of loans, operating budgets, seed money, emergency funds, building funds, equipment, matching funds, consulting services, technical assistance, program-related investments, special projects, publications, conferences, and seminars.

Focus of giving: Giving limited to South Eddy County, New Mexico.

$ Given: Expenditures: $249,513, including $62,853 for grants, $92,781 for grants to individuals, and $400,000 for one loan.

Assets: $2,464,031

Publications: Annual report, program policy statement, and application guidelines.

Contact: John Mills, Executive Director

*Incorporated in 1977 in New Mexico.

Walter Hightower Foundation
c/o El Paso National Bank
P. O. Drawer 140
El Paso, Texas 79980
(915) 546-6515

Restrictions: Giving in west Texas and southern New Mexico for health care for crippled children under the age of 21. Grants for general purposes, operating budgets, continuing support, annual campaigns, seed money, building funds, equipment, and program-related investments; grants also to individuals.

$ Given: $233,574 for grants: high $40,000.

Assets: $5,150,058

Contact: Terry Crenshaw, Charitable Services Officer
    Application information: application form required
    Initial approach: letter
    Copies of proposal: 2
    Deadline: July 1
    Board meeting date: annually
    Final notification: 2 months

NEW YORK

Mary Flagler Cary Charitable Trust
350 Fifth Avenue, Room 6622
New York, New York 10118
(212) 563-6860

Restrictions: Conservation of natural resources. Grants for operating budgets, continuing support, land acquisition, matching funds, special projects and program-related investments.

Focus of giving: Giving primarily in the New York City area and Eastern seaboard.

$ Given: $4,789,025 for 57 grants: high $100,000; low $3,000; average $44,000.

Assets: $73,366,533

Contact: Edward A. Ames, Trustee
    Initial approach: letter with brief proposal
    Copies of proposal: 1
    Deadlines: none
    Board meeting dates: usually every 3 weeks
    Final notification: 2 months

Cecil Charitable Trust
111 Broadway, Suite 512
New York, New York 10006

Restrictions: Grants primarily for historic preservation. Support for general purposes, seed money, special projects, conferences and seminars, matching funds,
and program-related investments.

Focus of giving: Giving primarily in New York and
Vermont.

$ Given: $111,950 for 55 grants: high $10,000; low
$100.

Assets: $1,196,880

Contact: George B. Cameron, Trustee
   Initial approach: letter
   Copies of proposal: 1
   Deadlines: April 1 and November 1
   Board meeting dates: May and December

Gebbie Foundation, Inc.
Hotel Jamestown Building, Room 308
Jamestown, New York 14701
(716) 487-1062

Restrictions: Grants for medical and scientific research
to alleviate human suffering and ills related to metabolic
diseases of the bone. Interested in programs of preven-
tive medicine as they relate to diseases of children, to
detection of deafness, and to training and education of
the deaf.

Focus of giving: Giving primarily in Jamestown; giving in other areas only when the project is consonant with program objectives that cannot be developed locally.

$ Given: $1,790,022 for 65 grants: high $201,000; low $140; average $1,000–$50,000.

Assets: $31,814,701

Contact: John D. Hamilton, President
>   **Initial approach:**   letter
>   **Copies of proposal:**   9
>   **Deadlines:**   none
>   **Board meeting dates:**   November, May, and September
>   **Final notification:**   1 to 4 months

A. Lindsay and Olive B. O'Connor Foundation
P.O. Box D
Hobart, New York 13788
(607) 538-9248

Restrictions: Broad purposes: local giving, with emphasis on "quality of life," including support for town, village, and environmental improvement.   Grants are awarded for general purposes, continuing support, seed money, emergency funds, building funds, equipment, land acquisition, special projects, publications, conferences and seminars, matching funds, loans, technical assistance, and program-related investments.

Focus of giving: Giving primarily in Delaware County, New York and contiguous rural counties in upstate New York.

$ Given: $1,262,964 for 45 grants: high $500,000; low $500; average $1,000–$20,000.

Contact: Donald F. Bishop, II, Executive Director

  Initial approach: letter

  Copies of proposal: 1

  Deadline: April 1

  Board meeting dates: May or June and September or October; committee meets monthly to consider grants under $5,000

  Final notification: 1 week to 10 days after semi-annual meeting

New York Foundation
350 Fifth Avenue, Room 2901
New York, New York 10118
(212) 594-8009

Restrictions: Giving for projects designed to improve the quality of life for disadvantaged, handicapped, and minority populations, with emphasis on youth and the elderly, especially projects with a strong community base.

Focus of giving: Giving primarily in the New York City metropolitan area.

$ Given: $1,613,000 for 80 grants: high $50,000; low $10,000; average $20,000.

Contact: Madeline Lee, Executive Director

  Initial approach: letter

  Copies of proposal: 1

  Deadlines: November 1, March 1, and July 1

Board meeting dates: February, June, and October

Final notification: 3 to 6 months

The Scherman Foundation, Inc.
315 West 57th Street, Suite 2D
New York, New York 10019
(212) 489-7143

Restrictions: Grants largely for conservation, disarmament and peace, family planning, human rights and liberties, the arts, and social welfare. Grants given for operating budgets, continuing support, seed money, emergency funds, matching funds, program-related investments, special projects, loans, and general purposes.

Focus of giving: Priority given to New York City organizations in the arts and social welfare fields.

$ Given: $2,119,000 for 153 grants: high $10,000; low $3,000; average $5,000–$25,000.

Assets: $38,061,969

Contact: David F. Freeman, Executive Director
    Initial approach: full proposal
    Copies of proposal: 1
    Deadlines: none
    Board meeting dates: quarterly
    Final notification: 3 months

The John Ben Snow Foundation, Inc.
P.O. Box 376
Pulaski, New York 13142
(315) 298-6401

Restrictions: Community betterment projects.

Focus of giving: Giving limited to central New York.

$ Given: $257,600 for 13 grants: high $45,000; low $1,000; average $3,500.

Assets: $3,175,900

Contact: Vernon F. Snow, President
> **Application information:** application form required
> **Initial approach:** letter
> **Copies of proposal:** 1
> **Deadline:** submit proposal between September and April; deadline is April 15
> **Board meeting date:** June

NORTH CAROLINA

Mary Reynolds Babcock Foundation, Inc.
102 Reynolds Village
Winston-Salem, North Carolina 27106-5123
(919) 748-9222

Restrictions: Broad purposes. Grants primarily for social services, including community development and youth employment, the environment, and citizen participation in the development of public policy. Grants for operating budgets, seed money, emergency funds, special projects, and program-related investments.

Focus of giving: Giving primarily in North Carolina and the southeastern United States.

$ Given: $3,127,491 for 156 grants; high $175,000; low $1,000; average $10,000–$50,000. Also $200,000 for two loans.

Assets: $40,601,750

Publications: Annual report, program policy statement, and application guidelines.

Contact: William L. Bondurant, Executive Director

    Application information: application form required

    Initial approach: letter, full proposal, or telephone

    Copies of proposal: 1

    Deadlines: submit proposal between December and February or June and August; deadlines March 1 and September 1

    Board meeting dates: May and November

    Final notification: first week of the month following a board meeting

Broyhill Foundation, Inc.
P.O. Box 700
Lenoir, North Carolina 28633

Restrictions: Local giving for civic and community services and the free enterprise system.

Focus of giving: Giving primarily in North Carolina.

$ Given: $573,059 for 244 grants: high $100,000; low $50; average $500–$5,000. Also $54,520 for 51 loans.

Assets: $18,697,186

Contact: Paul H. Broyhill, President
   Application information: application form required
   Initial approach: letter
   Board meeting dates: quarterly
   Final notification: within calendar year

James G. Hanes Memorial Fund/Foundation
c/o Wachovia Bank and Trust Company
P.O. Box 3099
Winston-Salem, North Carolina 27150
(919) 748-5269

Restrictions: Support for community programs.

Focus of giving: Giving primarily in North Carolina.

$ Given: $1,300,053 for 39 grants: high $125,000; low $1,000; average $1,000–$50,000.

Contact: E. Ray Cope, Vice President
   Application information: application form required
   Initial approach: proposal
   Copies of proposal: 1
   Deadlines: first day of month in which board meets; foundation prefers to receive applications in the preceding month
   Board meeting dates: January, April, July, and October.
   Final notification: 10 days

**The Kathleen Price and Joseph M. Bryan Family
Foundation, Inc.**
P.O. Box 1349
Greensboro, North Carolina 27402
(919) 379-7512

Restrictions: Grants for community projects, seed
money, building funds, and program-related investments.

Focus of giving: Giving primarily in North Carolina;
will also consider proposals from other states.

$ Given: $105,500 for 29 grants: high $10,000; low
$1,000; average $1,000–$10,000.

Assets: $1,566,000

Contact: Richard L. Wharton, Executive Secretary
  Initial approach: letter
  Copies of proposal: 1
  Deadlines: March 15 and September 15
  Board meeting dates: usually in March, May, and
  November
  Final notification: 3 months after board meeting

NORTH DAKOTA

Northwest Area Foundation
West 975 First National Bank Building
St. Paul, Minnesota 55101
(612) 224-9635

Restrictions: Grants generally for experimental and demonstration projects that promise significant impact on the community and the well-being of society but for which there is not now general support.

Focus of giving: Giving limited to an eight-state region that includes Idaho, Iowa, Minnesota, Montana, North Dakota, Oregon, South Dakota, and Washington.

$ Given: $6,967,105 for 196 grants: high $250,000; low $150; average $20,000–$60,000.

Contact: Terry Tinson, President

   Initial approach: telephone, letter, or proposal

   Copies of proposal: 2

   Deadlines: varies

   Board meeting dates: bimonthly, beginning in February

   Final notification: 60 to 90 days

NORTHEASTERN STATES

Ellis L. Phillips Foundation
13 Dartmouth College Highway
Lyme, New York 03768
(603) 795-2790

Restrictions: Support for education on public issues (particularly economic education) and for religion, historic preservation, conservation, and medical research. Grants for operating budgets, continuing support, annual campaigns, seed money, emergency funds, endowment funds, conferences, and seminars.

Focus of giving: Giving primarily in the northeastern United States.

$ Given: $268,658 for 45 grants: high $30,158; low $1,000; average $1,000–$10,000.

Assets: $4,198,892

Contact: Ellis L. Phillips, Jr. , President
  Initial approach: one- to three-page letter
  Copies of proposal: 1
  Board meeting dates: October, February, and May

OHIO

The William Bingham Foundation*
1250 Leader Building
Cleveland, Ohio 44114
(216) 781-3275

Restrictions: Grants for general purposes, special projects, seed money, building funds, equipment, publications, conferences and seminars, matching funds, and program-related investments.

Focus of giving: Giving primarily in the eastern United States, with some emphasis on the Cleveland, Ohio area.

$ Given: $640,244 for 27 grants: high $115,294; low $2,000; average $5,000–$30,000. Also $100,000 for one loan.

Assets: $16,137,000

*Incorporated in 1955 in Ohio.

Publications: Annual report, program policy statement, and application guidelines.

Donor: Elizabeth B. Blossom

Contact: Laura C. Hitchcox, Executive Director
 Initial approach: letter of two pages or less
 Copies of proposal: 1
 Deadlines: submit proposal preferably in February or July; deadline 2 months prior to board meeting dates
 Board meeting dates: usually May and October
 Final notification: 3 to 6 months

The Cleveland Foundation
1400 Hanna Building
Cleveland, Ohio 44115
(216) 861-3810

Restrictions: Grants are made to private tax-exempt and governmental agencies and programs serving the greater Cleveland area in the fields of civic and cultural affairs, education and economic development, and health and social services. Current priorities are in economic development; neighborhood development; downtown revitalization; lake front enhancement; programs dealing with the young, the aged, and special constituencies; and health care for the medically indigent and for underserved populations. Grants serve mainly as seed money for innovative projects or for developing institutions or services addressing unmet needs in the community. Very limited support for capital purposes for highly selective construction or equipment projects.

Focus of giving: Giving limited to the greater Cleveland area, with emphasis on Cleveland and Cuyahoga and Lake counties, Ohio, unless specified otherwise by donor.

$ Given: $17,100,149 for 675 grants: high $500,000; low $250; average $5,000–$50,000.

Contact: Steve A. Minter, Director

  Deadlines: March 31, June 15, August 31, and December 15

The Lorain Foundation
457 Broadway
Lorain, Ohio 44502

Restrictions: Grants for general purposes.

$ Given: $32,223 for grants.

Assets: $721,201

Contact: Edward J. Gould, Chairman

Marathon Oil Foundation, Inc.
539 South Main Street
Findlay, Ohio 45840
(419) 422-2121 Ext. 3708

Restrictions: Support for seed money, building funds, conferences and seminars, and program-related investments.

Focus of giving: Giving limited to areas of company operations.

$ Given: $1,789,407 for 368 grants: high $2,000,000; low $300. Also $197,778 for 50 grants to individuals.

Assets: $2,568,574

Contact: Carol Mittermaien, Assistant Secretary
    Initial approach: full proposal
    Copies of proposal: 1
    Deadlines: none
    Board meeting dates: as required
    Final notification: 6 to 8 weeks

Trust Corporation, Inc. Foundation
c/o Trust Corporation Bank, Ohio
Three Seagate
Toledo, Ohio 43603
(419) 259-8217

Restrictions: Charitable purposes: primarily local giving, with emphasis on community funds. Grants given for operating budgets, continuing support, emergency funds, building funds, equipment, land acquisition, consulting services, technical assistance, and program-related investments.

Focus on giving: Giving primarily in tristate area of Indiana, Michigan, and Ohio.

$ Given: $212,350 for 19 grants: high $148,000; low $100; average $1,000–$10,000.

Assets: $291,394

Contact: J. E. Lupe, Vice President
   Initial approach: letter
   Deadlines: none
   Board meeting dates: monthly
   Final notification: 2 months

The Leo Yassenoff Foundation
37 North High Street, Suite 304
Columbus, Ohio 43215
(614) 221-4315

Restrictions: Grants awarded for seed money, emergency funds, building funds, equipment, land acquisition, matching funds, consulting services, technical assistance, program-related investments, special projects, publications, conferences, seminars, and continuing support.

Focus of giving: Giving limited to the central Ohio area, with emphasis on Franklin County.

$ Given: $722,960 for 98 grants: high $200,000; low $200; average $1,000–$20,000.

Assets: $10,637,830

Contact: Cynthia Cecil Lazarus, Executive Director
   Initial approach: telephone, letter, or full proposal
   Copies of proposal: 1
   Deadlines: first business day of every other month, beginning in January
   Board meeting dates: every other month, beginning in January

OKLAHOMA

Phillips Petroleum Foundation, Inc.
Phillips Building, 16th Floor
Bartlesville, Oklahoma 74004
(918) 661-6248

Restrictions: Grants given for operating budgets, seed money, emergency funds, building funds, equipment, land acquisition, program-related investments, conferences and seminars, matching funds, and continuing support.

Focus on giving: Giving primarily in area of company operations.

$ Given: $3,595,030 for 712 grants: high $520,801; low $60.

Contact: John C. West, Executive Director
    Initial approach: proposal, letter, or telephone
    Copies of proposal: 1
    Deadlines: none
    Board meeting dates: January and as required
    Final notification: 6 to 8 weeks

OREGON

The Collins Foundation
909 Terminal Sales Building
Portland, Oregon 97205
(503) 227-1219

Restrictions: Grants are awarded for building funds, equipment, conferences and seminars, matching funds, program-related investments, land acquisition, and special projects.

Focus of giving: Giving limited to Oregon, with emphasis on Portland.

$ Given: $2,689,176, including $1,811,717 for 131 grants: high $250,000; low $725; average $2,500–$15,000.

Contact: William C. Pine, Executive Vice President
    Initial approach: letter
    Copies of proposal: 1
    Deadlines: none
    Board meeting dates: approximately 6 times a year
    Final notification: 2 months

The Jackson Foundation
c/o U. S. National Bank of Oregon
P.O. Box 3168
Portland, Oregon 97208
(503) 225-4461; (800) 547-1031 ex. 6558

Restrictions: Broad purposes: local giving, including funds for scientific research and technology.

Focus of giving: Giving limited to Oregon.

$ Given: $791,646 for 132 grants: high $64,200; low $300; average $2,000–$10,000. Also $764,330 for 18 loans.

Contact: Stephen W. Miller, Trust Officer
   Deadlines: none

Fred Meyer Charitable Trust
1515 Southwest Fifth Avenue, Suite 500
Portland, Oregon 97201
(503) 228-5512

Restrictions: Support for seed money, building funds, equipment, matching funds, technical assistance, program-related investments, special projects, and research.

Focus of giving: Support primarily in Oregon, with occasional grants at the initiative of the trust for programs in Washington, Idaho, Montana, and Alaska.

$ Given: $6,365,583 for 94 grants: high $555,000; low $964; average $20,000–$75,000.

Assets: $171,639,900

Contact: Charles S. Rooks, Executive Director

Application information: application form required

Initial approach: full proposal or letter

Copies of proposal: 1

Deadlines: no set deadlines, except for aging program

Board meeting dates: monthly

Final notification: 4 to 6 months for proposals that pass first screening; 2 to 3 months for those that do not

Northwest Area Foundation
West 975 First National Bank Building
St. Paul, Minnesota 55101
(612) 224-9635

Restrictions: Grants generally for experimental and demonstration projects that promise significant impact on the community and the well-being of society but for which there is not now general support.

Focus of giving: Giving limited to an eight-state region that includes Idaho, Iowa, Minnesota, Montana, North Dakota, Oregon, South Dakota, and Washington.

$ Given: $6,967,105 for 196 grants: high $250,000; low $150; average $20,000–$60,000.

Contact: Terry Tinson, President

  Initial approach: telephone, letter, or proposal

  Copies of proposal: 2

  Deadlines: varies

  Board meeting dates: bimonthly, beginning in February

  Final notification: 60 to 90 days

PENNSYLVANIA

Claude Worthington Benedum Foundation*
223 Fourth Avenue
Pittsburgh, Pennsylvania 15222
(412) 288-0360

Restrictions: Serves a broad variety of charitable purposes in West Virginia and southwestern Pennsylvania.
Funds are provided for projects that address regional
problems and needs, that establish demonstration projects with strong potential for replication in West Virginia, or that make outstanding contributions to the
area. Local initiatives and voluntary support are encouraged by the foundation.

Grants awarded for matching funds, consulting services, building funds, operating budgets, technical assistance, special projects, program-related investments,
and seed money.

$ Given: $5,646,092 for 73 grants: high $1,000,000;
low $2,500; average $75,000.

Assets: $108,939,234

Publications: Annual report and application guidelines.

Contact: Paul R. Jenkins, Executive Vice President

 Initial approach: letter

 Copies of proposal: 1

 Board meeting dates: March, June, September,
and December

 Final notification: 6 months

*Incorporated in 1944 in Pennsylvania.

Howard Heinz Endowment
CNG Tower, 30th Floor
625 Liberty Avenue
Pittsburgh, Pennsylvania 15222
(412) 391-5122

Restrictions: Local giving: usually with one-time, non-renewable grants for new programs, seed money, and capital projects.

Focus of giving: Giving limited to Pennsylvania, with emphasis on Pittsburgh and the Allegheny County area.

$ Given: $4,637,323 for 108 grants: high $500,000; low $500; average $5,000–$150,000.

Contact: Alfred W. Wishart, Jr., Executive Director
    Application information: application form required
    Initial approach: letter, full proposal, or telephone
    Copies of proposal: 1
    Deadlines: none
    Board meeting dates: spring and fall
    Final notification: 3 to 4 months

Kennametal Foundation
P.O. Box 231
Latrobe, Pennsylvania 15650
(412) 539-5203

Restrictions: Giving for general purposes, including community funds. Support for building funds, equipment, endowment funds, program-related investments, research, and matching funds.

$ Given: $129,283 for 100 grants: high $33,198; low $25.

Assets: $473,704

Contact: Richard Gibson, Secretary-Treasurer
    Initial approach: letter
    Copies of proposal: 1
    Deadlines: submit proposal preferably in January
    Board meeting dates: monthly

Richard King Mellon Foundation
525 William Penn Place
Pittsburgh, Pennsylvania 15219
(412) 392-2800

Restrictions: Grant programs emphasize conservation, medical research, and health care, largely in Pittsburgh and western Pennsylvania. Also interested in conservation of natural areas and wildlife preservation elsewhere in the United States. Grants awarded for seed money, building funds, equipment, land acquisition, endowment funds, research, matching funds, general purposes, and continuing support.

$ Given: $24,520,772 for 107 grants: high $9,000,000; low $2,500; average $10,000–$500,000.

Assets: $465,952,000

Contact: George H. Taber, Vice President
    Initial approach: full proposal
    Copies of proposal: 1

Deadlines: submit proposal between January and April or July and September; deadlines April 15 and October 15

Board meeting dates: June and December

**The Pittsburgh Foundation
CNG Tower, 30th Floor
265 Liberty Avenue
Pittsburgh, Pennsylvania 15222
(412) 391-5122**

Restrictions: Funds used largely locally, for programs to support special projects of regularly established agencies, capital and equipment needs, research of a non-technical nature, and demonstration projects.

Focus of giving: Giving limited to Pittsburgh and Allegheny County, Pennsylvania.

$ Given: $4,289,491 for 664 grants: high $150,000, low $37, average $5,000–$50,000.

Assets: $70,021,080

Contact: Alfred W. Wishart, Jr., Executive Director

Initial approach: letter, full proposal, or telephone

Copies of proposal: 1

Deadlines: 60 days prior to board meeting

Board meeting dates: March, June, September, and December

Final notification: 4 to 6 weeks

Williamsport Foundation
102 West Fourth Street
Williamsport, Pennsylvania 17701
(717) 326-2611

Restrictions: Charitable purposes: distribution of funds to serve the needs of Williamsport and vicinity. Grants given for building funds, emergency funds, equipment, general purposes, matching funds, program related investments, seed money, special projects, and loan.

$ Given: $899,945 for 84 grants: high $115,000; low $24; average $1,000–$30,000.

Assets: $16,821,254

Contact: Harold D. Hershberger, Jr., Secretary
   Initial approach: letter
   Copies of proposal: 5
   Deadlines: none
   Board meeting dates: at least 4 times a year
   Final notifications: 2 months

RHODE ISLAND

Old Stone Bank Charitable Foundation
180 South Main Street
Providence, Rhode Island 02903
(401) 278-2213

Restrictions: Broad purposes; local giving. Grants awarded for seed money, building funds, land acquisition, program-related investments, and special projects.

Focus of giving: Giving limited to Rhode Island.

$ Given: $238,798 for 24 grants: high $140,000; low $150.

Assets: $518,089

Contact: Kay H. Low, Manager
   Initial approach: letter or telephone
   Copies of proposal: 1
   Deadlines: first day of months when board meets
   Board meeting dates: bimonthly, beginning in January
   Final notification: 4 to 6 weeks

SOUTH DAKOTA

Northwest Area Foundation
West 975 First National Bank Building
St. Paul, Minnesota 55101
(612) 224-9635

Restrictions: Grants generally for experimental and demonstration projects that promise significant impact on the community and the well-being of society but for which there is not now general support.

Focus of giving: Giving limited to an eight-state region that includes Idaho, Iowa, Minnesota, Montana, North Dakota, Oregon, South Dakota, and Washington.

$ Given: $6,967,105 for 196 grants: high $250,000; low $150; average $20,000–$60,000.

Contact: Terry Tinson, President

Initial approach: telephone, letter, or proposal

Copies of proposal: 2

Deadlines: varies

Board meeting dates: bimonthly, beginning in February

Final notification: 60 to 90 days

SOUTHEASTERN STATES

Mary Reynolds Babcock Foundation, Inc.
102 Reynolds Village
Winston-Salem, North Carolina 27106-5123
(919) 748-9222

Restrictions: Broad purposes; grants primarily for social services, including community development and youth employment, the environment, and citizen participation in the development of public policy. Grants for operating budgets, seed money, emergency funds, special projects, and program-related investments.

Focus of giving: Giving primarily in North Carolina and the southeastern United States.

$ Given: $3,127,491 for 156 grants: high $175,000; low $1,000; average $10,000–$50,000. Also $200,000 for two loans.

Assets: $40,601,750

Publications: Annual report, program policy statement, and application guidelines.

Contact: William L. Bondurant, Executive Director

Application information: application form required

Copies of proposal: 1

Deadlines: submit proposal between December and February or June and August; deadlines March 1 and September 1

Board meeting dates: May and November

Final notification: first week of the month following a board meeting

---

TENNESSEE

Lyndhurst Foundation
701 Tallan Building
Chattanooga, Tennessee 37402
(615) 756-0767

Restrictions: Emphasis on health. Support for general purposes, seed money, matching funds, operating budgets, program-related investments, and special projects.

Focus of giving: Grants generally limited to Chattanooga.

$ Given: $2,827,077 for 50 grants: high $350,000; low $2,000; average $30,000–$150,000. Also $305,000 for 13 grants to individuals.

Assets: $91,695,737

Contact: Deaderick C. Montague, President

Application information: application form required for grants to individuals; awards made only at the initiative of the foundation

Initial approach: letter

Copies of proposal: 1

Deadlines: 4 weeks before board meetings; February 1 for Lyndhurst teachers, awards

Board meeting dates: February, May, August, and November

Final notification: 3 months

TEXAS

Communities Foundation of Texas, Inc.
4605 Live Oak Street
Dallas, Texas 75204
(214) 826-5231

Restrictions: Broad purposes: to promote the well-being of the inhabitants of Texas, primarily in the Dallas area. Support for operating budgets, annual campaigns, seed money, emergency funds, building funds, equipment, land acquisition, matching funds, consulting services, technical assistance, special projects, program-related investments, research, publications, conferences, and seminars.

Focus of giving: Giving primarily in the Dallas, Texas area.

$ Given: $11,310,838 for 925 grants: high $1,050,923; low $15; average $10,000–$25,000.

Assets: $89,520,522

Contact: Edward M. Fjorbak, Executive Vice President
   Initial approach: letter
   Copies of proposal: 1

Deadlines: 30 days before distribution committee meetings

Board meeting dates: distribution committee for unrestricted funds meets in March, August, and November

Final notification: 1 week after distribution committee meeting

Walter Hightower Foundation
c/o El Paso National Bank
P.O. Drawer 140
El Paso, Texas 79980
(915) 546-6515

Restrictions: Giving in west Texas and southern New Mexico for health care for crippled children under the age of 21. Grants for general purposes, operating budgets, continuing support, annual campaigns, seed money, building funds, equipment, and program-related investments. Grants also to individuals.

$ Given: $233,574 for grants: high $40,000.

Assets: $5,150,058

Contact: Terry Crenshaw, Charitable Services Officer
    Application information: application form required
    Initial approach: letter
    Copies of proposal: 2
    Deadline: July 1
    Board meeting date: annually
    Final notification: 2 months

Meadows Foundation, Inc.
Wilson Historic Block
2922 Swiss Avenue
Dallas, Texas 75204
(214) 826-9431

Restrictions: Support for operating budgets, continuing support, seed money, emergency funds, deficit
financing, building funds, equipment, land acquisition,
matching funds, special projects, publications, conferences and seminars, program-related investments, technical assistance, and consulting services.

Focus of giving: Giving limited to Texas, with emphasis on Dallas.

$ Given: $7,500,859 for 164 grants: high $1,000,000;
low $607; average $25,000–$50,000.

Assets: $324,123,001

Contact: Dr. Sally R. Lancaster, Executive Vice
President

    Initial approach: full proposal

    Copies of proposal: 1

    Deadlines: none

    Board meeting dates: April and November on
    major grants; grants review committee meets
    monthly

    Final notification: 3 to 4 months

Crystelle Waggoner Charitable Trust
c/o NCNB Texas
P.O. Box 1317
Forth Worth, Texas 76101
(817) 390-6925

Restrictions: Support for general purposes, annual campaigns, building funds, conferences and seminars, emergency funds, endowment funds, equipment, land acquisition, operating budgets, program-related investments, publications, research, seed money, special projects, and technical assistance.

Focus of giving: Giving limited to Texas, especially Fort Worth and Decatur.

$ Given: $339,922 for 33 grants: high $50,000; low $2,000; average $10,000.

Assets: $2,635,245

Contact: Darlene Mann, Vice President

  Initial approach: letter

  Copies of proposal: 1

  Deadlines: end of each quarter

  Board meeting dates: January, April, July, and October

  Final notification: 6 months, only if request is granted

VERMONT

Cecil Charitable Trust
111 Broadway, Suite 512
New York, New York 10006

Restrictions: Grants primarily for historic preservation. Support for general purposes, seed money, special projects, conferences and seminars, matching funds,
and program-related investments.

Focus of giving: Giving primarily in New York and
Vermont.

$ Given: $111,950 for 55 grants: high $10,000; low
$100.

Assets: $1,196,880

Contact: George B. Cameron, Trustee
   Initial approach: letter
   Copies of proposal: 1
   Deadlines: April 1 and November 1
   Board meeting dates: May and December

WASHINGTON

Northwest Area Foundation
West 975 First National Bank Building
St. Paul, Minnesota 55101
(612) 224-9635

Restrictions: Grants generally for experimental and demonstration projects that promise significant impact on the community and the well-being of society but for which there is not now general support.

Focus of giving: Giving limited to an eight-state region that includes Idaho, Iowa, Minnesota, Montana, North Dakota, Oregon, South Dakota, and Washington.

$ Given: $6,967,105 for 196 grants: high $250,000; low $150; average $20,000–$60,000.

Contact: Terry Tinson, President

   Initial approach: telephone, letter, or proposal

   Copies of proposal: 2

   Deadlines: varies

   Board meeting dates: bimonthly, beginning in February

   Final notification: 60 to 90 days

WEST VIRGINIA

Claude Worthington Benedum Foundation*
223 Fourth Avenue
Pittsburgh, Pennsylvania 15222
(412) 288-0360

Restrictions: Serves a broad variety of purposes in West Virginia and in southwestern Pennsylvania. Funds are provided for projects that address regional problems and needs, that establish demonstration projects with strong potential for replication in West Virginia, or that make outstanding contributions to the area. Local initiatives and voluntary support are encouraged by the foundation. Grants awarded for matching funds, consulting services, building funds, operating budgets, technical assistance, special projects, program-related investments, and seed money.

$ Given: $5,646,092 for 73 grants: high $1,000,000; low $2,500; average $75,000.

Assets: $108,939,234

Publications: Annual report and application guidelines.

Contact: Paul R. Jenkins, Executive Vice President
  Initial approach: letter
  Copies of proposal: 1
  Board meeting dates: March, June, September, and December
  Final notification: 6 months

*Incorporated in 1944 in Pennsylvania.

WISCONSIN

Judd S. Alexander Foundation, Inc.*
500 Third Street, Suite 509
P.O. Box 2137
Wausau, Wisconsin 54402-2137
(715) 845-4556

Restrictions: Grants for seed money, emergency funds, building funds, equipment, land acquisition, matching funds, technical assistance, and program-related investments.

Focus of giving: Giving primarily in Wisconsin.

$ Given: $270,472 for 56 grants: high $29,000; low $175. Also $157,723 for three loans.

Assets: $8,937,425

Publications: Application guidelines.

Contact: Stanley F. Staples, Jr., President
    Initial approach: letter, full proposal, or telephone
    Copies of proposal: 1
    Deadlines: none
    Board meeting dates: monthly
    Final notification: 60 days

*Incorporated in 1973 in Wisconsin.

Alvin R. Amundson Charitable Remainder Trust
c/o Marshall and Ilsley Bank, Madison Trust Office
P.O. Box 830
Madison, Wisconsin 53701

Restrictions: Local giving for community development.

Focus of giving: Giving limited to the village of Cambridge and surrounding municipalities.

$ Given: $68,225 for 12 grants: high $38,225;   low $1,000.

Assets: $1,083,756

Contact: Marshall and Ilsley Bank, Madison Trust Office

La Crosse Foundation
P.O. Box 489
La Crosse, Wisconsin 54602-0489
(608) 782-1148

Restrictions: Local giving for charitable purposes to benefit the citizens of La Crosse County, Wisconsin.

Focus of giving: Giving limited to La Crosse County, Wisconsin.

$ Given: $142,059 for 45 grants: high $30,000;   low $100; average $2,300. Also $9,816 for 20 grants to individuals.

Contact: Carol B. Popelka, Program Director
   Deadlines: submit proposal preferably 1 month before committee meetings

2

Program-Related Investments by Area of Business

AGRICULTURE

Butler Manufacturing Company Foundation*
BMA Tower, P.O. Box 917
Penn Valley Park
Kansas City, Missouri 64141
(816) 968-3000

Restrictions: Assistance for minorities and the handicapped, preservation of urban neighborhoods, development and improvement of agriculture and industry. Support for seed money, emergency funds, building funds, equipment, research, publications, matching funds, program-related investments, general purposes, and special projects.

$ Given: $281,427 for 102 grants, $74,166 for 38 grants to individuals, and $4,550 for five loans.

Assets: $2,431,279

* Incorporated in 1951 in Missouri.

Publications: Annual report, informational brochure, program policy statement, and application guidelines.

Donor: Butler Manufacturing Company

Contact: Barbara Fay

    Initial approach: telephone or letter

    Copies of proposal: 1

    Deadlines: submit proposal preferably in month prior to board meeting

    Board meeting dates: March, June, September, and December

    Final notification: 6 months

BUSINESS

Economic Development Administration (EDA)
U.S. Department of Commerce
14th and Constitution Avenue, N.W.
Washington, D.C. 20230
(202) 377-5113

Restrictions: To solve problems and remove roadblocks standing in the way of economic growth. Public and private nonprofit organizations, Indian tribes, individuals and/or profit enterprises are eligible to apply. Preference is given to projects assisting a designated redevelopment area, economic development district, or potential growth center. Nondesignated areas are eligible, however, if: (1) closing or imminent shutdown of a primary source of jobs is shown to have a major adverse effect on the area; (2) economic problems are so severe that the area is heading toward substantial unemployment in the near future; (3) the area is so closely linked, geographically or economically, with designated areas so as to substantially affect their economies; or (4) project focus is on solving a problem in a "hard hit" part of the area, with that section having persistent and substantial unemployment. The "Technical Assistance Program" includes management and operational assistance to firms as well as preliminary design and feasibility studies on development facilities. Grants may be used to employ personnel, hire consultants, contract for services, or in other ways provide for assistance in planning and carrying out action programs for economic progress.

$ Given: Technical assistance services are provided through direct EDA grants or via a grant to an intermediary organization with appropriate expertise. Although the federal share of such services may be 100 percent, a maximum nonfederal contribution is encouraged.

Technical assistance grants average $60,000. Grants should not exceed 75 percent of project costs. The nonfederal contribution for technical assistance grants may be in cash or kind. There were 151 awards given for fiscal year 1985.

Grants are usually for one year or less. Technical assistance may be renewed, however.

Contact: Official application materials are available upon request to the office at the address above or at EDA regional offices at Philadelphia, Atlanta, Chicago, Austin, Denver, and Seattle.

Address inquiries to: Director, Office of Planning, Technical Assistance Research and Evaluation

BUSINESS: CONSTRUCTION/EMPLOYMENT

Economic Development Administration (EDA)
U.S. Department of Commerce
14th and Constitution Avenue, N.W.
Washington, D.C. 20230
(202) 377-5113

Restrictions: The "Public Works Impact Program" (PWIP) is designed (1) to create immediate jobs through public works construction projects for the unemployed and underemployed and (2) to promote economic development in depressed areas.

$ Given:

> **Amount of support per award:** approximately $500,000

> **Matching fund requirements:** generally 20 percent to 50 percent of project costs

Contact: Applicant must first contact the Economic Development Representative for his or her area, then prepare a proposal for submittal to the regional office. If feasible, the regional office recommends to the national office for application authorization. Application must be initiated through the regional offices.

> **Regional officers:** John Corrigan, Director, Philadelphia Regional Office; Charles Oxley, Director, Atlanta Regional Office; William Roberts, Director, Denver Regional Office; Edward G. Jeep, Director, Chicago Regional Office; John Woodward, Director, Seattle Regional Office; and Hugh Farmer, Director, Austin Regional Office

> **Address inquiries to:** Christy Lay Bakaly, Special Assistant for Public Affairs, Room 7808, ED4

BUSINESS: EMPLOYMENT

The Edna McConnell Clark Foundation
250 Park Avenue, Room 900
New York, New York 10017
(212) 986-7050

Restrictions: Programs presently narrowly defined and directed toward five specific areas: (1) reducing unnecessary removal of children from troubled families by establishing better family preservation policies and services and by supporting courts, agencies, and advocates in implementation of specific foster care and adoption reforms; (2) improving the school-to-work transition of disadvantaged urban youth by developing model work-education programs among private industry, schools, community organizations, and unions and by monitoring government initiatives particularly as they relate to disadvantaged youth; (3) seeking more rational, humane, and effective ways of dealing with those in the criminal justice system by developing alternatives to unnecessary incarceration, supporting litigation to correct abuses and to establish standards of care, and exploring ways to reduce the length of prison sentences for offenders who present little threat to society; (4) helping millions in the developing world through a targeted research program aimed at controlling the tropical diseases schistosomiasis, trachoma, and onchocerciasis; and (5) care and welfare of the elderly.

$ Given: $14,065,132 for 140 grants: high $1,840,000; low $1,500; average $103,000.

Publications: Annual report, informational brochure, program policy statement, and application guidelines.

Contact: Peter D. Bell, President

  Initial approach: letter

  Copies of proposal: 1

  Deadlines: none

  Board meeting dates: February, April, June, September, and December

---

BUSINESS: FINANCE

Financial Executives Research Foundation
10 Madison Avenue
P.O. Box 1938
Morristown, New Jersey 07960
(201) 898-4600

Restrictions: To further the arts and sciences of all branches of controllership and treasurership and improve the usefulness of financial and accounting information.

Areas of interest include financial management and the evolving role of financial executives, the established practices of financial management, and the latest techniques to improve the effectiveness of the financial function.

Grants are made to support research projects in areas of interest to corporate financial management and with relevance to the entire financial and business community. Projects are expected to result in finished manuscripts acceptable for publication.

$ Given: Grants provide funds to cover all research costs of approved projects. In the past, research project support has ranged from $1,000 to over $100,000. The amount of support per award varies from project to project.

Contact: Roland L. Laing, Research Director

Number of awards: 6

Deadlines: applications may be submitted at any time and are considered on an individual basis

---

BUSINESS: IMPORT/EXPORT

International Trade Administration (ITA)
U.S. Department of Commerce
Room 4209, Main Commerce Building
Washington, D.C. 20230
(202) 377-0150

Restrictions: The "Trade Adjustment Technical Assistance Program" is designed to provide assistance to (1) trade-impacted firms that will assist those firms in maintaining a competitive position, save the jobs of current employees, and/or expand the level of employment to past peak levels; or to (2) trade or industry associations or other suitable organizations to enable a trade-injured industry to become more competitive with foreign competition.

Technical assistance grants and cooperative agreements are made to assist firms and industry or trade associations adversely affected by import competition. Technical services include assistance to examine economic alternatives, to develop a recovery strategy, or to otherwise prepare to deal with foreign competition.

Eligibility:

For firms: The firm must be certified by ITA's Office of Trade Adjustment Assistance, and this certification must still be current.

For trade or industry associations: The industry must show declining production/sales as well as evidence that imports are increasing in relation to domestic production in the industry; there must be Trade Act—certified firms in the industry; and/or the industry must have been declared import impacted by the International Trade Commission.

$ Given: Technical assistance services are provided through direct ITA grants or via a grant to an intermediary organization with appropriate expertise. ITA has established a national network of Trade Adjustment Assistance Centers (TAACs) to provide diagnostic and in-depth technical assistance to help eligible firms adjust to the problems caused by foreign competition. The TAACs employ professional staff and/or their contract with management and industry experts to provide management, export development, technology improvement, operations, and/or marketing assistance to such firms.

Total amount of support: $13.3 million estimated for the 1988 fiscal year

Representative awards: $1,200,000 to the New England Trade Adjustment Assistance Center, Inc., funding for the New England TAAC; $150,000 to the Gear Research Institute, for industrywide assistance to the gear manufacturers' industry

Contact: Information on the program, including application material and procedures, is available upon request to the Office of Trade Adjustment Assistance at the above address and phone number or at ITA-funded Trade Adjustment Assistance Centers (TAACs).

Address inquiries to: Deputy Assistant Secretary Office of Trade Adjustment Assistance (see address above)

BUSINESS: TECHNOLOGY

The Xerox Foundation
P.O. Box 1600
Stamford, Connecticut 06904
(203) 329-8700

Restrictions: To advance knowledge in science and technology; to enhance learning opportunities for minorities and the disadvantaged. Also operates employee matching gift program. Supports (1) social, civic, and cultural organizations, including United Way, providing broad-based programs and services in cities where Xerox employees live and work; (2) organizations that foster debate on major national public policy issues; and (3) worldwide, national leadership efforts around major social problems, education, conservation, and cultural affairs.

Grants awarded for general purposes, operating budgets, seed money, emergency funds, deficit financing, conferences and seminars, program-related investments, and consulting services.

Focus of giving: Giving primarily in areas of company operations.

$ Given: $8,500,000 for grants: high $1,145,500; low $250; average $5,000–$50,000.

Assets: $9,100,000

Contact: Robert W. Gudger, Vice President
   Initial approach: brief proposal
   Copies of proposal: 1
   Deadlines: none

Board meeting dates: usually in December and as required

Final notification: 3 months

COMMUNITY DEVELOPMENT

The New World Foundation
100 East 85th Street
New York, New York 10028
(212) 249-1023

Restrictions: The program places emphasis on (1) equal rights and opportunity, particularly on minority rights; (2) public education, especially the roles of parents and the community working together; (3) public health, particularly helping the disadvantaged, raising occupational health and safety standards, and reducing environmental hazards to health; (4) community initiative for rural and urban communities; and (5) avoidance of war, especially nuclear war, and seeking of peace.

$ Given: $1,579,700 for 145 grants: high $50,000; low $500; average $1,000–$25,000.

Contact: David Ramage, Jr., President

  Deadlines: none

  Board meeting dates: 3 times a year

  Final notification: 3 months

CONSERVATION

The Joyce Foundation
135 South LaSalle Street
Chicago, Illinois 60603
(312) 782-2464

Restrictions: Conservation and preservation of soil and water resources of the Midwest and Great Plains regions; and economic development—promotion of long-term employment opportunities for low-income individuals and communities.

Grants awarded for operating budgets, continuing support, seed money, emergency funds, matching funds, consulting services, technical assistance, program-related investments, loans, special projects, publications, conferences, and seminars.

Focus of giving: Giving primarily in the midwestern states, including Illinois, Indiana, Iowa, Michigan, Minnesota, Missouri, Ohio, and Wisconsin; limited number of conservation grants made in North Dakota, South Dakota, Kansas, and Nebraska.

$ Given: $6,310,857 for 279 grants: high $100,000; low $1,000; average $5,000–$50,000. Also $20,000 for two loans.

Assets: $200,037,648

Publications: Annual report, program policy statement, and application guidelines.

Donor: Beatrice Joyce Kean

Contact: Sheila Leahy, Senior Program Officer

Application information: application form required

Initial approach: letter

Copies of proposal: 1

Deadlines: January 15 for April meeting, Education, Economic Development; May 15 for August meeting, Health and Conservation; September 15 for December meeting, Culture and Government

Board meeting dates: April or May, August or September, and twice in December

Final notification: 3 weeks following meeting

The Xerox Foundation
P.O. Box 1600
Stamford, Connecticut
(203) 329-8700

Restrictions: To advance knowledge in science and technology; to enhance learning opportunities for minorities and the disadvantaged. Also operates employee matching gift program. Supports (1) social, civic, and cultural organizations, including United Way, providing broad-based programs and services in cities where Xerox employees live and work; (2) organizations that foster debate on major national public policy issues; and (3) worldwide, national leadership efforts around major social problems, education, conservation, and cultural affairs.

Grants awarded for general purposes, operating budgets, seed money, emergency funds, deficit financing, conferences and seminars, program-related investments, and consulting services.

Focus of giving: Giving primarily in areas of company operations.

$ Given: $8,500,000 for grants: high $1,145,500; low $250; average $5,000–$50,000.

Assets: $9,100,000

Contact: Robert W. Gudger, Vice President

> **Initial approach:**   brief proposal
>
> **Copies of proposal:**   1
>
> **Deadlines:**   none
>
> **Board meeting dates:**   usually in December and as required
>
> **Final notification:**   3 months

CONSERVATION/POPULATION

The Needmor Fund
1730 15th Street
Boulder, Colorado 80302
(303) 449-5801

Restrictions: Grants made without geographic restriction in the areas of environment and population.

> **Environment:**   On a national level, seeks to support nonadvocacy efforts to define the boundaries of current knowledge on the environment, to determine the areas where new knowledge is needed, or to ask critical questions concerning the environment in national and international dialogues. The fund is also interested in supporting organizations that are attempting to solve environmental problems that directly affect the lives of their members.

Population: Support for organizations that are examining the impact of population and/or developing new means of controlling and reducing population growth.

$ Given: $2,137,920, including $1,932,810 for 216 grants: high $200,000; low $25.

Assets: $4,564,701

Contact: Dinny Stranahan, Coordinator
    Initial approach: letter
    Deadlines: usually June 1 and December 1
    Board meeting dates: February and August
    Final notification: 2 weeks after board meeting

CONSTRUCTION

The Ford Foundation
320 East 43rd Street
New York, New York 10017
(212) 573-5000

Restrictions: To advance the public well-being by identifying and contributing to the solution of problems of national and international importance. Grants primarily to institutions and organizations for experimental, demonstrational, and developmental efforts that are likely to produce significant advances within the foundation's six major fields of interest: (1) urban poverty and the disadvantaged, (2) rural poverty and resources, (3) human rights and social justice, (4) education, (5) international politics and economic issues, and (6) governance and public policy.

$ Given: $113,102,009 for 1,510 grants: high $7,075,000; low $1,200; average $20,000–$200,000.

Publications: Annual report, newsletter, informational brochure, program policy statement, and application guidelines.

Contact: Barron M. Terry, Secretary

Initial approach: letter, full proposal, or telephone

Copies of proposal: 1

Deadlines: none

Board meeting dates: December, March, June, and September

Final notification: initial indication as to whether proposal falls within program interests within 1 month

ENERGY/ENVIRONMENTS

Max and Anna Levinson Foundation
1318 Beacon Street, Room 6
Brookline, Massachusetts 02146
(617) 731-1602

Restrictions: The development of a more humane and rewarding democratic society, in which people have greater ability and opportunity to determine directions for the future. Seeks to encourage projects that are concerned with promoting social change and social justice, either by developing and testing alternatives or by responsibly modifying existing systems, institutions, conditions, and attitudes that block promising innovation. Grants often given for projects of national and international impact in the areas of world peace, arms control, energy, environment, civil liberties, human rights, and the Jewish community. Support awarded for seed money, program-related investments, and special projects.

$ Given: $479,225 for 61 grants: high $25,000; low $500; average $500–$20,000.

Assets: $4,462,000

Publications: Informational brochure, application guidelines, and program policy statement.

Donors: Max Levinson, Carl A. Levinson

Contact: Sidney Shapiro, Executive Director
>   **Initial approach:** full proposal
>   **Copies of proposal:** 1
>   **Deadlines:** March 1 and September 1
>   **Board meeting dates:** May and November
>   **Final notification:** 2 weeks after board meeting

ENVIRONMENT

Charles Stewart Mott Foundation*
1200 Mott Foundation Building
Flint, Michigan 48502
(313) 238-5651

Restrictions: Supports community improvement through grants for expressing individuality, expanding personal horizons, community renewal, and environmental management. Support awarded for emergency

---

* Incorporated in 1926 in Michigan.

funds, loans, matching funds, operating budgets, program-related investments (only in the area of economic development), publications, seed money, special projects, conferences, and seminars.

$ Given: $26,513,612 for 356 grants: high $4,000,000; low $1,000; average $10,000–$200,000.

Assets: $569,037,725

Publications: Annual report, program policy statement, and application guidelines.

Contact: Jack Litzenberg, Vice President for Program Administration

    Initial approach: letter

    Copies of proposal: 1

    Deadlines: none

    Board meeting dates: March, June, September, and December

The New World Foundation
100 East 85th Street
New York, New York 10028
(212) 249-1023

Restrictions: The program places emphasis on (1) equal rights and opportunity, particularly on minority rights; (2) public education, especially the roles of parents and the community working together; (3) public health, particularly helping the disadvantaged, raising occupational health and safety standards, and reducing environmental hazards to health; (4) community initiative for rural and urban communities; and (5) avoidance of war, especially nuclear war, and seeking of peace.

$ Given: $1,579,700 for 145 grants; high $50,000; low $500; average $1,000–$25,000.

Contact: David Ramage, Jr., President
  Deadlines: none
  Board meeting dates: 3 times a year
  Final notification: 3 months

The Sherman Foundation, Inc.
315 West 57th Street, Suite 2D
New York, New York 10109
(212) 489-7143

Restrictions: Grants largely for conservation, disarmament and peace, family planning, human rights and liberties, the arts, and social welfare.
  Grants given for operating budgets, continuing support, seed money, emergency funds, matching funds, program-related investments, special projects, loans, and general purposes.

Focus of giving: Priority given to New York City organizations in the arts and social welfare fields.

$ Given: $2,119,000 for 153 grants: high $10,000; low $3,000; average $5,000–$25,000.

Assets: $38,061,969

Contact: David F. Freeman, Executive Director
  Initial approach: full proposal
  Copies of proposal: 1

Deadlines: none

Board meeting dates: quarterly

Final notification: 3 months

The Shalan Foundation, Inc.
10 Lombard Street, Suite 250
San Francisco, California 94111
(415) 438-4545

Restrictions: Giving primarily in western states except for projects of national importance; interest in groups promoting economic change to increase social justice and to limit practices harmful to the environment. Grants awarded for general purposes, operating budgets, continuing support, matching funds, and program-related investments.

$ Given: $342,150 for 26 grants: high $20,000; low $3,000; average $10,000–$20,000.

Assets: $1,139,091

Contact: Catherine Lerza, Executive Director

    Initial approach: brief description or full proposal

    Deadlines: March, July, and November

    Final notification: 1 to 3 months

HEALTH

Adrian & Jessie Archbold Charitable Trust*
Chemical Bank, Administrative Services Department
30 Rockefeller Plaza, 60th Floor
New York, New York 10012
(212) 621-2143

Restrictions: Grants primarily for hospitals and health-related organizations. Grants awarded for general purposes, continuing support, program-related investments, research, publications, conferences, and seminars.

$ Given: Expenditures $812,395, including $684,074 for 164 grants: high $235,000; low $100.

Assets: $10,488,788

Donor: Mrs. Adrian Archbold

Contact: Barbara Strohmeier, Vice President
    Initial approach: proposal
    Copies of proposal: 1
    Board meeting dates: as required
    Final notification: 3 to 6 months

The John A. Hartford Foundation, Inc.
35 East 59th Street, 23rd Floor
New York, New York 10022
(212) 832-7788

* Trust established in 1976 in New York.

Restrictions: Broad purposes in health care

Health Care Financing Program: Grants to improve the effectiveness of the health care system by stimulating the payment system and associated organizational reforms.

Aging and Health Program: Grants to address specific needs of the elderly, including improved diagnostic techniques and coordination of care for long-term, chronic health problems.

Hartford Geriatric Faculty Development Awards Program: Provides retraining of physicians who are planning academic careers in geriatrics.

John A. and George L. Hartford Fellowship Program: Grants to train and develop young physicians who wish to pursue careers in medical research.

Grants given for operating budgets, continuing support, program-related investments, fellowships, special projects, research, publications, conferences and seminars, and loans.

$ Given: $4,160,842 for 52 grants: high $207,514; low $5,000. Also $1,323,000 for 35 grants to individuals.

Assets: $155,170,232

Contact: Steven Eyre, Executive Director

Initial approach: proposal in three to four pages (for Health Care Financing and Aging and Health programs)

Copies of proposal: 2

Deadlines: none

Board meeting date: December

Final notification: 1 month

The Robert Wood Johnson Foundation
P.O. Box 2316
Princeton, New Jersey 08543
(609) 452-8701

Restrictions: Improvement of health services in the United States, with emphasis on projects to improve access to personal health care of the most underserved population groups. Purpose is to make health care arrangements more effective and affordable and to help people maintain or regain maximum attainable function in their everyday lives. Within these areas, support provided for the development and testing of previously untried approaches, demonstrations to assess objectively the operational effectiveness of approaches shown to be effective in more limited settings, and the broader diffusion of programs objectively shown to improve health status or make health care more affordable. Grants given for seed money, research, special projects, and continuing support.

Focus of giving: Giving limited to the United States.

$ Given: $57,737,244 for 208 grants: high $1,194,608; low $5,319.

Assets: $1,173,836,335

Contact: Edward H. Robbins, Proposal Manager
    Initial approach: letter
    Copies of proposal: 1
    Deadlines: none
    Board meeting dates: February, May, July, October, and December

INTERNATIONAL: LATIN AMERICA

Vollmer Foundation, Inc.
217 Gravel Hill Road
Kinnelan, New Jersey 07405
(201) 492-2309

Restrictions: Support for activities dedicated primarily to Venezuela. Grants given for annual campaign, seed money, equipment, program-related investments, general purposes, and continuing support.

$ Given: $716,856 for 29 grants; high $132,530; low $1,650. Also $19,305 for two grants to individuals.

Assets: $6,822,074

Contact: Albert L. Ennist, Assistant Secretary
   Initial approach: letter
   Copies of proposal: 2
   Deadlines: submit proposal preferably between December and March
   Board meeting dates: as required
   Final notification: 2 to 3 months

INTERNATIONAL TRADE/ INTERNATIONAL FINANCE

Rockefeller Brothers Fund
1290 Avenue of the Americas
New York, New York 10104
(212) 397-4800

Restrictions: "Support of efforts in the United States and abroad that contribute ideas, develop leaders, and

encourage institutions in the transition to global inter-
dependence and that counter world trends of resource
depletion, militarization, protectionism, and isolation
which now threaten to move humankind everywhere further away from cooperation, trade and economic growth,
arms restraint, and conservation." There are four major
giving categories: (1) "One World," with two major components: resources management and security, including
issues related to arms control and those involving international relations, development, trade, and finance, (2)
New York City, (3) the well-being of the nonprofit sector,
and (4) "special concerns."

Focus of giving: No support for churches, hospitals,
or community centers. No grants to individuals or for
endowments or building.

$ Given: $26,208,888 for 143 grants: high:
$15,000,000; low $2,000; average $10,000–$75,000.

Contact: Benjamin R. Shute, Jr., Secretary

   Initial approach: letter, full proposal, or telephone

   Copies of proposal: 1

JOB DEVELOPMENT

Norman Foundation, Inc.
215 East 62nd Street
New York, New York 10021
(212) 230-9800

Restrictions: Major interests include the protection of
civil rights and civil liberties and, in general, broaden-
ing and improving the quality of citizen participation
in the political, economic, and social processes of U.S.
communities. A major portion of grants are currently

being made to projects that address the economic plight of the working and nonworking poor and that enable them to have more voice in the institutions that allocate jobs and resources in their communities. Grants awarded for general purposes, matching funds, seed money, and special projects.

Focus of giving: Giving limited to the United States.

$ Given: $360,250 for 62 grants: high $25,000; low $100; average $7,500–$15,000.

Assets: $12,903,112

Contact: Jody Adams Weisbrod, Program Director
>   **Initial approach:**   letter or full proposal
>   **Copies of proposal:**   1
>   **Deadlines:**   none
>   **Board meeting dates:**   quarterly
>   **Final notification:**   1 to 5 months

MINORITIES

Butler Manufacturing Company Foundation*
BMA Tower, P.O. Box 917
Penn Valley Park
Kansas City, Missouri 64141
(816) 968-3000

* Incorporated in 1951 in Missouri.

Restrictions: Assistance for minorities and the handicapped, preservation of urban neighborhoods, development and improvement of agriculture and industry. Support for seed money, emergency funds, building funds, equipment, research, publications, matching funds, program-related investments, general purposes, and special projects.

$ Given: $281,472 for 102 grants, $74,166 for 38 grants to individuals, and $4,550 for five loans.

Assets: $2,431,279

Publications: Annual report, informational brochure, program policy statement, and application guidelines.

Donor: Butler Manufacturing Company

Contact: Barbara Fay
   Initial approach: telephone or letter
   Copies of proposal: 1
   Deadlines: submit proposal preferably in month prior to board meeting
   Board meeting dates: March, June, September, and December
   Final notification: 6 months

O.P. & W.E. Edwards Foundation, Inc.
Hearthstone Village
South Londonderry, Vermont 05155
(802) 824-3770

Restrictions: Major interest in programs helping at-risk youth become able to survive and thrive on their own, with preference to smaller, comprehensive programs.

$ Given: $431,334 for 45 grants: high $50,000; low $500; average $5,000–$10,000.

Contact: David E. Gamper, President
    Initial approach: letter
    Copies of proposal: 1
    Deadlines: none
    Board meeting dates: as required
    Final notification: 1 to 2 months

The New World Foundation
100 East 85th Street
New York, New York 10028
(212) 249-1023

Restrictions: The program places emphasis on (1) equal rights and opportunity, particularly on minority rights; (2) public education, especially the roles of parents and the community working together; (3) public health, particularly helping the disadvantaged, raising occupational health and safety standards, and reducing environmental hazards to health; (4) community initiative for rural and urban communities; and (5) avoidance of war, especially nuclear war, and seeking of peace.

$ Given: $1,579,700 for 145 grants: high $50,000; low $500; average $1,000–$25,000.

Contact: David Ramage, Jr., President
   Deadlines: none
   Board meeting dates: 3 times a year
   Final notification: 3 months

MINORITIES: EMPLOYMENT

The Joyce Foundation
135 South LaSalle Street
Chicago, Illinois 60603
(312) 782-2464

Restrictions: Conservation and preservation of soil and water resources of the Midwest and Great Plains regions; and economic development—promotion of long-term employment opportunities for low-income individuals and communities.

Grants awarded for operating budgets, continuing support, seed money, emergency funds, matching funds, consulting services, technical assistance, program-related investments, loans, special projects, publications, conferences, and seminars.

Focus of giving: Giving primarily in the midwestern states, including Illinois, Indiana, Iowa, Michigan, Minnesota, Missouri, Ohio, and Wisconsin; limited number of conservation grants made in North Dakota, South Dakota, Kansas, and Nebraska.

$ Given: $6,310,857 for 279 grants: high $100,000; low $1,000; average $5,000–$50,000. Also $20,000 for two loans.

Assets: $200,037,648

Publications: Annual report, program policy statement, and application guidelines.

Donor: Beatrice Joyce Kean

Contact: Charles U. Daly, President

Application information: application form required

Initial approach: letter

Copies of proposal: 1

Deadlines: January 15 for April meeting, Education, Economic Development; May 15 for August meeting, Health and Conservation; September 15 for December meeting, Culture and Government

Board meeting dates: April or May, August or September, and twice in December

Final notification: 3 weeks following meeting

NATURAL RESOURCES

The Ford Foundation
320 East 43rd Street
New York, New York 10017
(212) 573-5000

Restrictions: To advance the public well-being by identifying and contributing to the solution of problems of national and international importance. Grants primarily to institutions and organizations for experimental, demonstrational, and developmental efforts that are likely to produce significant advances within the Foundation's six major fields of interest: (1) urban poverty and the disadvantaged, (2) rural poverty and resources,

(3) human rights and social justice, (4) education, (5) international politics and economic issues, and (6) governance and public policy.

$ Given: $113,102,009 for 1,510 grants: high $7,075,000; low $1,200; average $20,000–$200,000.

Publications: Annual report, newsletter, informational brochure, program policy statement, and application guidelines.

Contact: Barron M. Terry, Secretary
> **Initial approach:** letter, full proposal, or telephone
> **Copies of proposal:** 1
> **Deadlines:** none
> **Board meeting dates:** December, March, June, and September
> **Final notification:** initial indication as to whether proposal falls within program interests within 1 month

OCCUPATIONAL SAFETY AND HEALTH

National Institute for Occupational Safety and Health
1600 Clifton Road, N.E.
Atlanta, Georgia 30333
(404) 329-3343

Restrictions: Grants are awarded to conduct investigations into the underlying characteristics and causes of occupational safety and health problems and for effective solutions in dealing with them.

Grants are also awarded to conduct pilot or full-scale programs that will effectively determine and demonstrate the technical or economic feasibility or application of a new or improved occupational safety or health procedure, method, technique, or system.

$ Given: Grants of $120,000, $20,000, and $32,000.

Contact: Application forms are mailed upon request from the office below.

Address inquiries to:
Centers for Disease Control
NIOSH Grants Program
Building 1, Room 3051
Atlanta, Georgia 30333

Deadlines: new applications: February 1, June 1, October 1

POPULATION/CONSERVATION

The Needmor Fund
1730 15th Street
Boulder, Colorado 80302
(303) 449-5801

Restrictions: Grants made without geographic restriction in the areas of environment and population.

Environment: On a national level, seeks to support nonadvocacy efforts to define the boundaries of current knowledge on the environment, to determine the areas where new knowledge is needed, or to ask critical questions concerning the environment in national and international dialogues. The fund is also interested in supporting organizations that are attempting to solve environmental problems that directly affect the lives of their members.

Population: Support for organizations that are examining the impact of population and/or developing new means of controlling and reducing population growth.

$ Given: $2,137,920, including $1,932,810 for 216 grants: high $200,000; low $25.

Assets: $4,564,701

Contact: Dinny Stranahan, Coordinator
> **Initial approach:** letter
> **Deadlines:** usually June 1 and December 1
> **Board meeting dates:** February and August
> **Final notification:** 2 weeks after board meeting

REAL ESTATE

Charles Stewart Mott Foundation*
1200 Mott Foundation Building
Flint, Michigan 48502
(313) 238-5651

Restrictions: Supports community improvement through grants for expressing individuality, expanding personal horizons, community renewal, and environmental management. Support awarded for emergency funds, loans, matching funds, operating budgets, program-related investments, publications, seed money, special projects, conferences, and seminars.

---

* Incorporated in 1926 in Michigan.

$ Given: $26,513,612 for 356 grants: high $4,000,000; low $1,000; average $10,000–$200,000.

Assets: $569,037,725

Publications: Annual report, program policy statement, and application guidelines.

Contact: Jack Litzenberg, Vice President for Program Administration

> **Initial approach:** letter
>
> **Copies of proposal:** 1
>
> **Deadlines:** none
>
> **Board meeting dates:** March, June, September, and December

The Windham Foundation, Inc.
P.O. Box 70
Grafton, Vermont 05146
(802) 843-2211

Restrictions: A private operating foundation in which 85 percent of adjusted net income is applied to operating programs of the foundation, including civic improvement and historic preservation. The foundation's primary activity is the preservation of properties in rural areas of Vermont to maintain their charm and historic, native, or unusual features, with emphasis on restoration of houses in Grafton. The remaining 15 percent of the foundation's income is used for general charitable giving.

Focus of giving: Giving limited to Vermont, with emphasis on Windham County.

$ Given: $230,641 for 57 grants: high $30,000; low $100. Also $116,590 for 357 grants to individuals.

Contact: Stephan A. Morse, Executive Director
  Initial approach: letter
  Copies of proposal: 1
  Deadlines: none
  Board meeting dates: February, May, July, and October
  Final notification: following the board meeting

URBAN DEVELOPMENT

Butler Manufacturing Company Foundation*
BMA Tower, P.O. Box 917
Penn Valley Park
Kansas City, Missouri 64141
(816) 968-3000

Restrictions: Assistance for minorities and the handicapped, preservation of urban neighborhoods, development and improvement of agriculture and industry. Support for seed money, emergency funds, building funds, equipment, research, publications, matching funds, program-related investments, general purposes, and special projects.

$ Given: $281,472 for 102 grants, $74,166 for 38 grants to individuals, and $4,550 for five loans.

---

* Incorporated in 1951 in Missouri.

Assets: $2,431,279

Publications: Annual report, informational brochure, program policy statement, and application guidelines.

Donor: Butler Manufacturing Company

Contact: Barbara Fay

Initial approach: telephone or letter

Copies of proposal: 1

Deadlines: submit proposal preferably in month prior to board meeting

Board meeting dates: March, June, September, and December

Final notification: 6 months

FLOW-THROUGH FUNDING

The grants in this section consist of cash awards, consulting services, and technical assistance. There is also loan information contained within this section. Most of these foundations will not fund individuals or businesses directly, but instead will only give money to enterprises that are designated as charitable under section 501(c)(3) of the Internal Revenue Code. However, you as an individual or business can work through a nonprofit organization, which will act as your sponsor or parent organization. The monies given to you are paid directly to the nonprofit organization, which in turn pays you. Usually the nonprofit organization receives a fee of between three and seven percent of monies raised. There is NO upfront fee paid to the sponsor or parent organization; the three to seven percent fee is customary, it is not an obligation.

How do you go about finding a nonprofit conduit? Check any local directory of nonprofit organizations available (your local library will usually have such directories in its collection, perhaps in a community services section). Contact local citywide consortium-styled associations that operate in your area of interest, such as the United Way, arts councils, health and welfare planning bodies, federations, and so on. Speak to their directors or public information officers and elicit their suggestions for possible sponsors. Also check national organizational reference books, such as the *Encyclopedia of Associa-*

tions, for other potential candidates.

This section also includes grants that take the form of donated services. Technical assistance, consulting services, and other donated services can be an invaluable help to a new or existing business. I have also included community foundations in this section that serve a wide variety of local needs.

3

Flow-Through Funding by State

ARKANSAS

Winthrop Rockefeller Foundation
308 East Eighth Street
Little Rock, Arkansas 72202
(501) 376-6854

Restrictions: Broad purposes: emphasis on economic development and education. Support for local projects that (1) improve the delivery of services of administrative capacity of institutions; (2) increase the participation of people in the decision-making process; or (3) achieve more productive development and use of human, physical, and fiscal resources. The foundation will fund innovative demonstration projects that improve people's living standards and the institutions that serve the community; projects that have economic development potential; and community-based projects concerned with organizational planning and fund raising. Support is available for special projects, seed money, conferences and seminars, matching funds, technical assistance, and consulting services.

Focus of giving: Giving primarily in Arkansas or to projects that benefit Arkansas.

$ Given: $1,294,884 for 54 grants: high $222,695; low $450; average $10,000–$40,000.

Publications: Annual report, program policy statement, and application guidelines.

Contact: Thomas C. McRae, President

Application information: application form required

Initial approach: telephone or letter

Copies of proposal: 2

Deadlines: submit proposal preferably 8 weeks prior to meeting

Board meeting dates: on the first weekend in March, June, September, and December

Final notification: 2 weeks after board meeting dates

CALIFORNIA

California Community Foundation*
3580 Wilshire Boulevard, Suite 1660
Los Angeles, California 90010
(213) 413-4042

Restrictions: Grants for matching funds, technical assistance, special projects, and employee matching gifts.

Focus of giving: Giving limited to Los Angeles, Orange, Riverside, San Bernadino, and Ventura counties in California.

*California Community Foundation established in 1915 in California by bank resolution.

$ Given: $3,719,458 for 226 grants: high $64,540; low $100; average $5,000–$20,000. Also $1,261 for 24 employee matching gifts.

Publications: Annual report, application guidelines, and informational brochure.

Contact: Jack Shakely, Executive Director
   Initial approach: full proposal
   Copies of proposal: 1
   Deadlines: none
   Board meeting dates: quarterly
   Final notification: 3 months after board meets

Community Foundation of Santa Clara County
960 West Hedding, Suite 220
San Jose, California 95126
(408) 241-2666

Restrictions: Grants for seed money, emergency funds, matching funds, employee matching gifts, consulting services, and technical assistance.

Focus of giving: Giving primarily in Santa Clara County, California.

$ Given: $478,438 for 144 grants: high $43,684; low $50.

Publications: Annual report and application guidelines.

Contact: Marti Erickson, Executive Director
   Application information: application form required
   Initial approach: telephone

Deadlines: 8 weeks prior to board meetings

Board meeting dates: 2nd Friday of January, May, and September

Final notification: within 2 weeks of meetings

Evelyn and Walter Haas, Jr. Fund*
1090 Sansome Street, Third Floor
San Francisco, California 94111
(415) 544-6575

Restrictions: Grants for seed money, equipment, special projects, technical assistance, and general purposes.

Focus of giving: Giving primarily in the San Francisco Bay Area, California.

$ Given: $1,165,246 for 95 grants: high $225,000; average $5,000–$50,000.

Publications: Annual report, program policy statement, and application guidelines.

Contact: Melissa Bannett, Executive Director

    Initial approach: letter

    Copies of proposal: 1

    Deadlines: none

    Board meeting dates: March, June, September, and December

    Final notification: within 90 days

*Incorporated in 1953 in California.

Peninsula Community Foundation
1204 Burlingame Avenue
P.O. Box 627
Burlingame, California 94011-0627
(415) 342-2477

Restrictions: To support local cultural, educational, social service, and health programs. Interests include youth, environment, elderly, disabled, civic concerns, and recreation. Also provides counseling services for local fund seekers. Support for operating budgets, continuing support, seed money, emergency funds, equipment, matching funds, consulting services, technical assistance, loans, special projects, research, publications, conferences, and seminars.

Focus of giving: Giving limited to San Mateo County and northern Santa Clara County, California.

$ Given: $867,456 for 258 grants: high $67,166; low $25; average $5,000–$20,000. Also $29,000 for one foundation-administered program.

Publications: Annual report, application guidelines, informational brochure, and grants list.

Contact: Bill Somerville, Executive Director

  Initial approach: letter

  Copies of proposal: 1

  Deadlines: none

  Board meeting dates: distribution committee meets in January, March, May, July, September, and November

  Final notification: 3 months

San Diego Community Foundation
525 B Street, Suite 410
San Diego, California 92101
(619) 239-8815

Restrictions: Support for seed money, equipment, matching funds, technical assistance, research, conferences, and seminars

Focus of giving: Giving limited to San Diego County, California.

$ Given: $537,430 for 85 grants: high $50,000; low $165.

Publications: Annual report, application guidelines, and program policy statement.

Contact: Helen Monroe, Executive Director, or Pamela Hall, Program Officer

> **Application information:** application form required

> **Initial approach:** telephone or letter

> **Copies of proposal:** 1

> **Deadlines:** January 1, February 1, June 1, and October 1

> **Board meeting dates:** bimonthly, beginning in February

> **Final notification:** 2 months

L. J. Skaggs and Mary C. Skaggs Foundation*
1221 Broadway, 21st Floor
Oakland, California 94612
(415) 451-3300

*Incorporated in 1967 in California.

Restrictions: Grants for seed money, special projects, matching funds, technical assistance, general purposes, and continuing support.

Focus of giving: Giving primarily in northern California for social and community careers grants.

$ Given: $1,225,960 for 150 grants: high $125,000; low $100; average $5,000–$25,000.

Publications: Annual report, program policy statement, application guidelines, and grants list.

Contact: Philip M. Jelley, Foundation Manager, or David J. Knight, Program Director

Initial approach: letter

Copies of proposal: 1

Deadlines: June 1 for letter of intent, September 1 for proposal

Board meeting date: November

Final notification: 2 to 3 weeks after board meeting

COLORADO

The Anschutz Family Foundation
2400 Anaconda Tower
555 17th Street
Denver, Colorado 80202
(303) 293-2338

Restrictions: Grants for special projects, operating budgets, continuing support, annual campaigns, seed money, emergency funds, consulting services, technical assistance, research, publications, conferences, and seminars.

Focus of giving: Giving primarily in Colorado, especially Denver.

$ Given: $825,230 for 67 grants: high $75,000; low $2,000; average $5,000–$50,000.

Publications: 990-PF and application guidelines.

Contact: Sue Redgers, Executive Director

> **Application information:** grants awarded in November
>
> **Initial approach:** letter
>
> **Deadlines:** submit proposal preferably in May through September; deadline October 1
>
> **Board meeting dates:** spring and October
>
> **Final notification:** 1 week to 6 months

CONNECTICUT

Aetna Life and Casualty Foundation, Inc.*
151 Farmington Avenue
Hartford, Connecticut 06105
(203) 273-2240

Restrictions: Support for operating budgets, continuing support, seed money, emergency funds, matching funds, employee matching gifts, and technical assistance.

Focus of giving: Giving limited to organizations in the United States, with emphasis on the greater Hartford, Connecticut area.

---

*Incorporated in 1972 in Connecticut.

$ Given: $8,260,957 for 421 grants: high $632,000; average $5,000–$20,000. Also $866,068 for 698 employee matching gifts.

Publications: Annual report, application guidelines, and program policy statement.

Contact: Marge Mlodzinski, Program Officer
   Initial approach: letter
   Copies of proposal: 1
   Deadlines: none
   Board meeting dates: February, May, August, and November
   Final notification: 2 months

The Bridgeport Area Foundation, Inc.
446 University Avenue
Bridgeport, Connecticut 06604
(203) 334-7511

Restrictions: Broad purposes: grants to organizations and for projects that primarily benefit the communities of Bridgeport, Easton, Fairfield, Milford, Monroe, Shelton, Stratford, Trumbull, and Westport. Grants for continuing support, annual campaigns, seed money, emergency funds, building funds, equipment, consulting services, technical assistance, conferences, seminars, and special projects.

$ Given: $437,125 for 285 grants: high $64,000; low $100; average $3,000–$5,000.

Publications: Annual report, program policy statement, and application guidelines.

Contact: Ronald D. Williams, Chairman, Distribution
Committee

    Initial approach: letter

    Copies of proposal: 4

    Deadline: September

    Board meeting dates: April and October; distribution committee meets in March, June, September, and December

    Final notification: 2 weeks after committee meetings

Hartford Foundation for Public Giving*
85 Gillett Street
West Hartford, Connecticut 06105
(203) 548-1888

Restrictions: Grants for seed money, emergency funds, building funds, equipment, land acquisition, matching funds, loans, and special projects.

Focus of giving: Giving limited to the greater Hartford, Connecticut area.

$ Given: $4,513,261 for 167 grants: high $271,062; low $383; average $40,000–$50,000.

Publications: Annual report, application guidelines, and program policy statement.

Contact: R. Malcolm Salter, Director

    Application information: application required

    Initial approach: telephone

*Community foundation established in 1925 in Connecticut by resolution and declaration of trust.

Copies of proposal: 3

Deadlines: none

Board meeting dates: monthly, except August

Final notification: 60 to 90 days

DISTRICT OF COLUMBIA

The Community Foundation of Greater Washington, Inc.*
1002 Wisconsin Avenue, N.W.
Washington, D.C. 20007
(202) 338-8993

Restrictions: Support for seed money, emergency funds, technical assistance, program-related investments, special projects, research, publications, conferences, and seminars.

Focus of giving: Giving limited to the metropolitan Washington, D.C. area.

$ Given: $792,896 for 101 grants: high $104,128; low $250. Also $441,248 for three foundation-administered programs.

Publications: Annual report, program policy statement, application guidelines, informational brochure, and newsletter.

Contact: Joan Bridges, Grants Coordinator

  Initial approach: letter

  Copies of proposal: 1

*Community foundation incorporated in 1973 in the District of Columbia.

Deadlines: none

Board meeting dates: March, June, and November

Final notification: up to 3 months

HAWAII

The Hawaiian Foundation
111 South King Street
P.O. Box 3170
Honolulu, Hawaii 96802
(808) 525-8548

Restrictions: Grants for operating budgets, continuing support, seed money, deficit financing, equipment, matching funds, technical assistance, research, special projects, and publications.

Focus of giving: Giving primarily in Hawaii.

$ Given: $357,395 for 61 grants and $28,686 for 75 grants to individuals.

Publications: Program policy statement, application guidelines, informational brochure, and annual report.

Contact: Mark J. O'Donnell, Trust Officer

Application information: application forms required for grants to individuals

Initial approach: telephone or proposal

Copies of proposal: 9

Deadlines: 1st day of month preceding board meeting

Board meeting dates: January, April, July, and October

ILLINOIS

The Chicago Community Trust*
222 North LaSalle Street, Suite 1400
Chicago, Illinois 60601
(312) 372-3356

Restrictions: Grants for operating budgets, continuing support, seed money, emergency funds, building funds, equipment, land acquisition, matching funds, research, and special projects.

Focus of giving: Giving primarily in Cook County, Illinois.

$ Given: $19,301,203, including $17,310,895 for grants.

Publications: Annual report, informational brochure, program policy statement, and application guidelines.

Contact: Trinita Logue, Assistant Director
    Initial approach: full proposal
    Copies of proposal: 2
    Deadlines: none
    Board meeting dates: March, June or July, September, and December
    Final notification: 90 days after board meeting

*Community foundation established in 1915 in Illinois by bank resolution and declaration of trust.

Patrick and Anna M. Cudahy Fund*
P.O. Box 11978
Milwaukee, Wisconsin 53211
(414) 962-6820

Restrictions: Grants for general purposes, operating budgets, continuing support, annual campaigns, seed money, emergency funds, deficit financing, building funds, equipment, land acquisition, matching funds, consulting services, technical assistance, special projects, research, publications, conferences and seminars, and fellowships.

Focus of giving: Giving primarily in Wisconsin and Chicago, Illinois and for national programs.

$ Given: $876,660 for 116 grants: high $50,000; low $400; average $1,000–$10,000.

Publications: Application guidelines.

Contact: Jane Ramsey, Director
 Initial approach: letter
 Copies of proposal: 1
 Deadlines: 1 month prior to board meetings
 Board meeting dates: usually in March, June, September, and December
 Final notification: 1 week after meeting

W. Clement and Jessie V. Stone Foundation
111 East Wacker Drive, Suite 510
Chicago, Illinois 60601
(312) 565-1100

*Incorporated in 1949 in Wisconsin.

Restrictions: Broad purposes: "making this world a better place in which to live" through programs that seek to put a "Positive Mental Attitude" philosophy into action in the areas of education, mental health, religion, and youth work. Money for consulting services and technical assistance.

$ Given: $118,325 for 28 grants: high $15,000; low $80; average $5,000.

Publications: Annual report and informational brochure.

Contact: Maree G. Bullock, Executive Director

> **Application information:**   funds presently committed, but consulting services are available; application form required
>
> **Initial approach:** letter
>
> **Copies of proposal:** 1
>
> **Deadlines:** none
>
> **Board meeting dates:** April
>
> **Final notification:** 90 days

INDIANA

Irwin-Sweeney-Miller Foundation*
420 Third Street
P.O. Box 808
Columbus, Indiana 47202
(812) 372-0251

---

*Incorporated in 1952 in Indiana.

Restrictions: Grants for conferences, seminars, continuing support, operating budgets, seed money, technical assistance, and special projects.

Focus of giving: Giving limited to the Columbus, Indiana area for all new funding.

$ Given: $652,155 for 44 grants: high $249,900; low $100; average $2,000–$5,000.

Publications: Biennial report.

Contact: Susan Ingmire, Program Officer
    Initial approach: letter or full proposal
    Copies of proposal: 1
    Deadlines: March 1 and September 1
    Board meeting dates: April and October
    Final notification: 1 month

KANSAS

The Sosland Foundation*
P.O. Box 29155
Shawnee Mission, Kansas 66201
(913) 236-7300

Restrictions: Grants for general purposes, operating budgets, continuing support, annual campaigns, seed money, emergency funds, deficit financing, building funds, equipment, land acquisition, endowment funds, matching funds, consulting services, and technical assistance.

*Incorporated in 1955 in Missouri.

$ Given: $319,178 for 84 grants: high $100,000; low $25; average $1,000–$4,000.

Focus of giving: Giving primarily in Missouri.

Contact: Ron Heiligman, Philanthropic Consultant
Initial approach: letter
Deadlines: none
Board meeting dates: March, June, September, and December
Final notification: 3 months

KENTUCKY

Greater Ashland Foundation, Inc.*
1212 Bath Avenue
P.O. Box 2096
Ashland, Kentucky 41105
(606) 324-3888

Restrictions: Support for operating budgets, continuing support, seed money, emergency funds, consulting services, and technical assistance.

Focus of giving: Giving limited to the tristate area of Ashland, Kentucky; Ironton, Ohio; and Huntington, West Virginia.

$ Given: Expenditures: $291,741.

Publications: Annual report.

Contact: Linda L. Ball, Executive Director

*Community foundation incorporated in 1972 in Kentucky.

Application information: application form required

Initial approach: letter

Copies of proposal: 1

Board meeting date: June

The Louisville Community Foundation, Inc.*
Meidinger Tower, Suite 101
Louisville, Kentucky 40202
(502) 585-4649

Restrictions: Grants for consulting services, technical assistance, seed money, special projects, and emergency funds. Primarily human services.

Focus of giving: Giving limited to the greater Louisville, Kentucky area.

$ Given: $107,224 for 26 grants: high $37,000; low $450; average $4,000–$6,000.

Publications: Annual report, program policy statement, and application guidelines.

Contact: Darrell L. Murphy, Executive Director

   Application information: application form required

   Initial approach: letter

   Copies of proposal: 10

   Deadlines: January 1

   Board meeting dates: September, December, March, and June

---

*Established in 1916 in Kentucky; reorganized in 1984.

LOUISIANA

The Greater New Orleans Regional Foundation*
2515 Canal Street, Suite 404
New Orleans, Louisiana 70119
(504) 822-4906
Restrictions: Grants for emergency funds, technical assistance, seed money, and special projects.

Focus of giving: Giving limited to the greater New Orleans, Louisiana area.

$ Given: $26,299 for 10 grants.

Publications: Annual report, application guidelines, and program policy statement.

Contact: Patricia Mason, Executive Director
  Application information: application form required
  Initial approach: proposal

MARYLAND

Morris Goldseker Foundation of Maryland, Inc.**
5 East Read Street
Baltimore, Maryland 21202
(301) 837-5100

*Established in 1924 in Louisiana, as the Community Chest; became a community foundation in 1983.
**Incorporated in 1973 in Maryland.

Restrictions: Support for seed money, emergency funds, matching funds, consulting services, technical assistance, and special projects.

Focus of giving: Giving limited to the Baltimore, Maryland area.

$ Given: $3,141,759, including $922,601 for 32 grants: high $54,000; low $5,000.

Publications: Annual report, program policy statement, and application guidelines.

Contact: Timothy D. Armbruster, Executive Director
  Application information: submit preliminary letter as early as possible before deadlines
  Initial approach: brief letter
  Copies of proposal: 1
  Deadlines: April 1, August 1, and December 1
  Board meeting dates: distribution committee meets 3 times a year in March, June, and October
  Final notification: after board meeting

MASSACHUSETTS

The Henry P. Kendall Foundation*
One Boston Place
176 Federal Street
Boston, Massachusetts 02110
(617) 951-2525

*Trust established in 1957 in Massachusetts.

Restrictions: Grants for operating budgets, seed money, emergency funds, research, special projects, publications, conferences, seminars, and continuing support.

$ Given: $1,861,111 for 84 grants: high $480,585; low $600; average $1,000–$50,000.

Publications: Program policy statement and application guidelines.

Contact: Robert L. Allen, Vice President
   Initial approach: letter
   Copies of proposal: 1
   Deadlines: none
   Board meeting dates: as required
   Final notification: 2 months

The Arthur D. Little Foundation*
25 Acorn Park
Cambridge, Massachusetts 02140
(617) 864-5770

Restrictions: Grants for continuing support, annual campaigns, seed money, emergency funds, deficit financing, research, special projects, publications, conferences and seminars, consulting services, and technical assistance. Giving in areas of higher education, community services, and health care.

Focus of giving: Giving primarily in areas of company operations.

$ Given: $418,798 for 132 grants: high $75,000; low $300.

*Trust established in 1953 in Massachusetts.

Publications: Program policy statement and application guidelines.

Contact: Joan Behre, Secretary for the Trustees
　　Initial approach: letter
　　Copies of proposal: 2
　　Deadlines: none
　　Board meeting dates: May and October

MICHIGAN

Grand Rapids Foundation*
209-C Waters Building
161 Ottawa NW
Grand Rapids, Michigan 49503
(616) 454-1751

Restrictions: Support for seed money, emergency funds, building funds, equipment, land acquisition, matching funds, and scholarship funds.

Focus of giving: Giving limited to Kent County, Michigan.

$ Given: $1,122,617 for 55 grants: high $123,300; low $83; average $500–$100,000. Also $51,904 for grants to individuals and $80,500 for 37 loans.

Publications: Annual report, informational brochure, program policy statement, and application guidelines.

Contact: Diana Sieger, Executive Director
　　Application information: application form required

---

*Community foundation established in 1922 in Michigan by resolution and declaration of trust.

Initial approach: letter or telephone

Copies of proposal: 10

Deadlines: submit student loan applications between January 1 and April 1; deadline for all other applications 4 weeks preceding board meeting

Board meeting dates: bimonthly, beginning in August

Final notification: 1 month

The Jackson Foundation*
505 Wildwood Avenue
Jackson, Michigan 49201
(517) 787-1321

Restrictions: Money for general purposes, support for community improvement, and other programs for the benefit of the residents of Jackson County. Grants also for seed money, building funds, equipment, land acquisition, matching funds, consulting services, technical assistance, loans, special projects, and research.

Focus of giving: Giving limited to Jackson County, Michigan.

$ Given: $146,402 for 11 grants: high $75,000; low $500; average $500–$3,000.

Publications: Annual report.

Contact: Jody Bacon, Executive Director

    Application information: application form required

    Initial approach: letter or telephone

    Copies of proposal: 1

*Community foundation incorporated in 1948 in Michigan.

Deadlines: submit proposal preferably in January, April, July, or October; deadlines February 1, May 1, August 1, and November 1

Board meeting dates: March, June, September, and December

Final notification: 6 weeks

Muskegon County Community Foundation, Inc.*
Frauenthal Center, Suite 304
407 West Western Avenue
Muskegon, Michigan 49440
(616) 722-4538

Restrictions: Grants for seed money, special projects, matching funds, building funds, equipment, land acquisition, research, publications, conferences and seminars, endowment funds, and annual campaigns.

Focus of giving: Giving limited to Muskegon County, Michigan.

$ Given: $373,094 for 46 grants: high $58,600; low $200; average $1,000–$5,000. Also $163,259 for 192 grants to individuals.

Publications: Annual report and application guidelines.

Contact: Patricia B. Johnson, Executive Director
    Application information: application form required
    Initial approach: letter or telephone
    Copies of proposal: 12

*Community foundation incorporated in 1961 in Michigan.

Deadlines: January, April, July, or October

Board meeting dates: February, May, August, and November

Final notification: 2 to 3 weeks

The Simpson Foundation*
c/o City Bank & Trust Company
One Jackson Square
Jackson, Michigan 49201
(517) 788-2711

Restrictions: Grants for seed money, emergency funds, building funds, equipment, matching funds, consulting services, technical assistance, and special projects.

Focus of giving: Giving limited to Hillsdale County or to programs benefiting Hillsdale County, Michigan.

$ Given: $100,445 for grants: average $10,000.

Contact: Robert E. Carlson, Vice President and Trust Officer

Application information: application form required

Initial approach: full proposal, letter, or telephone

Deadlines: submit proposal preferably in August or September

Board meeting date: October

Final notification: 30 to 60 days

*Established in 1980 in Michigan.

MINNESOTA

Dayton Hudson Foundation*
777 Nicollet Mall
Minneapolis, Minnesota 55402
(612) 370-6553

Restrictions: Money for operating budgets, continuing support, annual campaigns, building funds, equipment, matching funds, consulting services, technical assistance, special projects, and publications.

Focus of giving: Giving primarily in areas of company operations; grants rarely given for national organizations or programs.

$ Given: $11,018,720 for 789 grants: high $1,000,000; low $250; average $1,000–$5,000.

Publications: Company report, informational brochure, program policy statement, and application guidelines.

Contact: Vivian K. Stuck, Administrative Officer

> **Application information:** organizations located outside Minnesota should apply to local headquarters office of Dayton Hudson Corporation
>
> **Initial approach:** letter with proposal
>
> **Copies of proposal:** 1
>
> **Deadlines:** none
>
> **Board meeting dates:** March, June, September, and December
>
> **Final notification:** within 60 days, although decisions are generally not made between January 31 and April 15

*Incorporated in 1917 in Minnesota.

The Minneapolis Foundation*
500 Foshay Tower
821 Marquette Avenue
Minneapolis, Minnesota 55402
(612) 339-7343

Restrictions: Grants for seed money, emergency funds, equipment, technical assistance, and special projects.

Focus of giving: Giving primarily in the Minneapolis-St. Paul, Minnesota seven-county metropolitan area.

$ Given: $2,596,126 for 534 grants: high $50,000; low $50; average $5,000–$15,000.

Publications: Annual report, application guidelines, and program policy statement.

Contact: Marion Etzwiler, Executive Director

Application information: undesignated funds considered in June and December; requests to the McKnight-Neighborhood Self-Help Initiatives Program reviewed in March and September; application form required

Initial approach: letter or telephone

Copies of proposal: 14

Deadlines: 6 weeks before distribution committee meeting

Board meeting dates: semiannually; distribution committee meets quarterly

Final notification: 4 months

*Community foundation incorporated in 1915 in Minnesota.

Rochester Area Foundation*
First Bank Building, Suite 406
201 S.W. First Avenue
Rochester, Minnesota 55902
(507) 282-0203

Restrictions: To help launch new projects that represent innovative approaches to community needs, support special purposes of established organizations, promote volunteer and citizen involvement in the community, respond to current human needs in the community, and support projects without other sources of support. Giving in areas of health, education, social services, and civic and cultural affairs. Grants available for seed money, emergency funds, building funds, equipment, matching funds, technical assistance, conferences, and seminars.

Focus of giving: Giving limited to Olmsted County, Minnesota.

$ Given: $63,436 for 20 grants.

Publications: Annual report, program policy statement, and application guidelines.

Contact: Ann Downing, Executive Director
  Application information: application form required
  Initial approach: letter
  Copies of proposal: 11
  Deadlines: submit proposals in January, April, July, and October
  Board meeting dates: February, May, August, and November

*Community foundation established in 1944 in Minnesota by resolution of trust.

Final notification: 1 week

MISSOURI

Edward F. Swinney Trust*
127 West Tenth Street, Suite 406
Kansas City, Missouri 64105
(816) 842-0944

Restrictions: Giving for demonstration and experimental projects, extension and improvement of human services, with preference in the voluntary sector; for planning and cooperation among voluntary agencies and between public and private agencies; and for education and training in community services. Grants for operating budgets, seed money, emergency funds, consulting services, technical assistance, special projects, research, publications, conferences, and seminars.

Focus of giving: Giving limited to Missouri.

$ Given: $253,265 for 12 grants: high $180,000; low $2,000; average $25,000–$50,000.

Publications: Annual report, application guidelines, and program policy statement.

Contact: Dalene Bradford, Vice President-Programs
  Initial approach: letter or full proposal
  Copies of proposal: 1
  Deadline: December 2
  Board meeting dates: 1st Tuesday in April, July, October, and December
  Final notification: 10 days after board meetings

*Trust established in 1946 in Missouri.

NEW HAMPSHIRE

The New Hampshire Charitable Fund*
One South Street
P.O. Box 1335
Concord, New Hampshire 03302-1335
(603) 255-6641

Restrictions: Grants for seed money, loans, general purposes, special projects, and grants to individuals.

Focus of giving: Giving limited to New Hampshire.

$ Given: $1,239,056 for 354 grants: high $207,966; low $78. Also $187,428 for 205 grants to individuals and $349,636 for 175 loans.

Publications: Annual report, program policy statement, application guidelines, and newsletter.

Contact: Deborah Cowan, Associate Director
    Initial approach: telephone
    Deadlines: February 1, May 1, August 1, and November 1
    Board meeting dates: March, June, September, and December
    Final notification: 4 to 6 weeks

*Community foundation incorporated in 1962 in New Hampshire.

NEW JERSEY

The Prudential Foundation
15 Prudential Plaza
Newark, New Jersey 07101
(201) 802-7354

Restrictions: Program interests include business and economic research and education, conservation and ecology, culture, education, health, public affairs, and urban and community affairs. Grants for operating budgets, continuing support, annual campaigns, seed money, emergency funds, deficit financing, building funds, equipment, matching funds, employee matching gifts, consulting services, technical assistance, research, and special projects.

Focus of giving: Giving primarily in areas of company operations, especially Newark, New Jersey.

$ Given: $5,657,381 for 600 grants: high $198,000; low $1,000; average $5,000–$10,000. Also $1,179,918 for 4,000 employee matching gifts.

Publications: Annual report and application guidelines.

Contact: Donald N. Trloar, Secretary

> **Application information:** additional information will be requested as needed
>
> **Initial approach:** letter with brief description of program
>
> **Copies of proposal:** 1
>
> **Deadlines:** none

Board meeting dates: March, June, September, and December

Final notification: 4 to 6 weeks

Victoria Foundation, Inc.
40 South Fullerton Avenue
Montclair, New Jersey 07042
(201) 783-4450

Restrictions: Grants primarily for local welfare and education programs, including urban problems, neighborhood development, youth agencies, and behavioral rehabilitation; support also for certain statewide environmental projects. Grants for operating budgets, continuing support, seed money, emergency funds, deficit financing, building funds, matching funds, special projects, research, consulting services, and technical assistance.

Focus of giving: Giving primarily in the greater Newark, New Jersey area.

$ Given: 141 grants: high $65,000; low $5,000; average $10,000–$25,000.

Publications: Annual report and application guidelines.

Contact: Howard E. Quirk, Executive Officer

    Application information: application form required

    Initial approach: proposal

    Copies of proposal: 1

    Deadlines: submit proposal in January through March or June through September; deadlines March 15 and September 15

Board meeting dates: May and December

Final notification: within 1 week after board meeting if accepted; within 30 days after board meeting if not accepted

NEW YORK

Albany's Hospital for Incurables*
P.O. Box 3628, Executive Park
Albany, New York 12203
(518) 459-7711

Restrictions: Money for general purposes, building funds, equipment, land acquisition, and matching funds.

Focus of giving: Giving limited to Albany, Schenectady, Rensselaer, and Saratoga counties, New York.

$ Given: $166,150 for 16 grants: high $25,000; low $5,000. Also $19,106 for one loan.

Publications: Annual report, program policy statement, and application guidelines.

Contact: Arnold Cogswell, President
　　Application information: application form required
　　Initial approach: telephone, letter, or full proposal
　　Deadlines: 30 days before board meetings
　　Board meeting dates: January, April, June, and September
　　Final notification: 5 days after board meets

*Established in 1974 in New York.

Stewart W. & Wilma C. Hoyt Foundation
300 Security Mutual Building
80 Exchange Street
Binghamton, New York 13901
(607) 722-6706

Restrictions: Grants for general purposes, building funds, matching funds, seed money, special projects, operating budgets, continuing support, emergency funds, equipment, technical assistance, consulting services, conferences, and seminars.

Focus of giving: Giving limited to Broome County, New York.

$ Given: $461,260 for 41 grants: high $100,000; low $1,400; average $1,500–$30,000.

Publications: Annual report, informational brochure, program policy statement, and application guidelines.

Contact: Judith C. Peckham, Executive Director

   Application information: no grants considered at January meeting

   Initial approach: telephone or letter

   Copies of proposal: 1

   Deadlines: 1st day of month prior to board meetings

   Board meeting dates: bimonthly, beginning in January

   Final notification: 1 to 3 days following board meetings

Bruner Foundation, Inc.*
244 Fifth Avenue
New York, New York 10001
(212) 889-5366

Restrictions: Primarily local giving. Historically, aid has been given to innovative programs, particularly for health care and public health/preventive medicine, including care for the aged. In the future, the foundation will continue to make limited grants in these areas; however, the emphasis will be on projects involving children and adolescents and racial and religious intergroup relations. Funds are primarily for the evaluation of projects; the foundation is actively involved in improving the assessment of the impact of social programs.

Focus of giving: Giving primarily in New York.

$ Given: $496,100 for 18 grants: high $98,000; low $5,000; average $5,000–$50,000.

Publications: Multiyear report, program policy statement, and application guidelines.

Contact: Janet Carter, Executive Director

> **Initial approach:** letter and brief outline of proposal, including budget
>
> **Copies of proposal:** 1
>
> **Deadlines:** none
>
> **Board meeting dates:** as required
>
> **Final notification:** 1 month

---

*Incorporated in 1963 in New York.

The Buffalo Foundation
237 Main Street
Buffalo, New York 14203
(716) 852-2857

Restrictions: Grants for operating budgets, seed money, emergency funds, building funds, equipment, land acquisition, special projects, matching funds, consulting services, technical assistance, research, publications, conferences, seminars, and general purposes.

Focus of giving: Giving primarily in Erie County, New York.

$ Given: $1,289,111 for 123 grants: high $109,050; low $78. Also $245,263 for 421 grants to individuals.

Publications: Annual report and application guidelines.

Contact: W. L. Van Schoonhoven, Director

> **Application information:** application forms for scholarship applicants only, must be requested between March 1 and May 10
>
> **Initial approach:** proposal
>
> **Copies of proposal:** 1
>
> **Deadlines:** March 31, June 30, September 30, or December 31 for grants; May 25 for scholarships
>
> **Board meeting dates:** 1st Wednesday of February, May, August, and November
>
> **Final notification:** 1st meeting after submission

Fund for the City of New York, Inc.
419 Park Avenue South, 16th Floor
New York, New York 10016
(212) 689-1240

Restrictions: A private operating foundation supporting public and private projects designed to improve the effectiveness of government and the quality of life in New York City, with particular emphasis on public service productivity, accountability, performance monitoring, and computer assistance; operates a program of assistance to public managers; also runs a cash flow loan program against governmental grants and contracts. Money for technical assistance and loans.

Focus of giving: Giving limited to the New York City area.

$ Given: $306,875 for 35 grants: high $50,000; low $500. Also $1,672,127 for 31 foundation-administered programs.

Publications: Multiyear report, 990-PF, program policy statement, and application guidelines.

Contact: Anita Nager, Grants Administrator
    Initial approach: full proposal
    Copies of proposal: 1
    Deadlines: none
    Board meeting dates: approximately 5 times a year in December, February, April, June, and September

The Glens Falls Foundation
55 Colvin Ave.
Albany, NY 12206
(518) 793-6302

Restrictions: Broad purposes, including the promotion of the mental, moral, and physical improvement of the people of Glens Falls and environs. Grants for seed money, emergency funds, building funds, equipment, research, publications, conferences and seminars, special projects, matching funds, consulting services, technical assistance; grants also to individuals.

Focus of giving: Giving limited to Warren, Washington, and Saratoga counties, New York. No grants for endowment funds; no loans.

$ Given: $73,369 for 29 grants: high $10,000; low $35. Also $7,500 for 27 grants to individuals.

Contact: Robert Gibeault, Administrator

Initial approach: letter, telephone, or full proposal

Copies of proposal: 8

Deadlines: submit proposal preferably in December, March, June, or September; deadline 1st day of months in which board meets

Board meeting dates: 2nd Wednesday in January, April, July, and October

Final notification: 2 days after quarterly meetings

The J. M. Kaplan Fund, Inc.
330 Madison Avenue
New York, New York 10017
(212) 661-8485

Restrictions: Interest primarily in programs in architecture and urban planning; preservation, parks, and other urban amenities; local cultural institutions and selected arts projects; and certain civil liberties and human needs programs. Support also for trustee matching gifts program. Grants for employee matching gifts, continuing support, seed money, emergency funds, matching funds, special projects, publications, and technical assistance.

Focus of giving: Giving primarily in New York, with emphasis on New York City.

$ Given: $3,324,800 for 117 grants: high $250,000; low $1,000; average $20,000. Also $448,500 for 35 employee matching gifts.

Publications: Annual report and application guidelines.

Contact: Joan K. Davidson, President

  Initial approach: telephone, full proposal, or letter

  Copies of proposal: 1

  Deadlines: submit proposal only from March to November; deadline November 1

  Board meeting dates: as required

  Final notification: 2 months

The New York Community Trust*
415 Madison Avenue
New York, New York 10017
(212) 758-0100

Restrictions: Grants for seed money, matching funds, employee matching gifts, consulting services, technical assistance, special projects, research, publications, conferences, and seminars.

Focus of giving: Giving limited to New York, New York.

$ Given: $37,239,322 for 3,780 grants: high $1,000,000; low $100; average $20,000–$25,000.

Publications: Annual report, program policy statement, application guidelines, and newsletter.

Contact: Herbert B. West, Director, or Richard Mittenthal, Assistant Director of Programs

    Initial approach: full proposal

    Copies of proposal: 1

    Deadlines: none

    Board meeting dates: February, April, June, July, October, and December

    Final notification: 4 months

The Frederick W. Richmond Foundation, Inc.
245 East 58th Street, Suite 10-A
New York, New York 10022
(212) 752-1668

---

*Community foundation established in 1923 in New York by resolution and declaration of trust.

Restrictions: Grants for special projects and seed money.

Focus of giving: No grants to individuals.

$ Given: $199,427 for 40 grants: high $37,500; low $150; average $1,000. Also $20,025 for three loans.

Publications: 990-PF and program policy statement.

Contact: Timothy E. Wyman, President
   Initial approach: letter
   Copies of proposal: 1
   Deadlines: none
   Board meeting dates: September and March
   Final notification: 3 months

Stern Fund*
370 Lexington Avenue
New York, New York 10017
(212) 532-0617

Restrictions: Broad purposes: to foster democracy and social and institutional responsiveness in the public and private arenas of the United States. To this end, seeks to identify and support energetic, strategically rational, theoretically well-grounded efforts to effect appropriate institutional development or change; to develop new ways of life and work; to redress the imbalances and inequities of American life; and to defend existing constitutional and institutional protections of freedom. Grants for seed money, matching funds, research, publications, special projects, general purposes, and loans.

*Incorporated in 1936 in Louisiana

Focus of giving: No grants to individuals, or for building or endowment funds.

$Given: $363,500 for 21 grants: high $40,000, low $2,000.

Publications: Application guidelines.

Contact:

   Initial approach: full proposal or letter

   Copies of proposal: 1

   Deadlines: none

   Board meeting dates: semiannually in the fall and spring

   Final notification: within 3 weeks if proposal is not considered

NORTH CAROLINA

Foundation for the Carolinas
301 South Brevard Street
Charlotte, North Carolina 28202
(704) 376-9541

Restrictions: Support for operating budgets, seed money, emergency funds, building funds, equipment, matching funds, consulting services, technical assistance, land acquisition, special projects, and research.

Focus of giving: Giving primarily in North Carolina and South Carolina.

$ Given: $2,385,853 for 1,225 grants: high $209,800; low $100; average $500–$10,000. Also $12,398 for 15 grants to individuals and $4,000 for four loans.

Publications: Annual report, application guidelines, informational brochure, and newsletter.

Contact: William Spencer, President
   Application information: application form required
   Initial approach: letter
   Copies of proposal: 11
   Deadlines: none
   Board meeting dates: quarterly, with annual meeting in March; distribution committee meets monthly
   Final notification: 1 to 2 months

OHIO

Greater Ashland Foundation, Inc.*
1212 Bath Avenue
P.O. Box 2096
Ashland, Kentucky 41105
(606) 324-3888

Restrictions: Grants for operating budgets, continuing support, seed money, emergency funds, consulting services, and technical assistance.

Focus of giving: Giving limited to the tri-state area of Ashland, Kentucky; Ironton, Ohio; and Huntington, West Virginia.

$ Given: Expenditures: $291,741.

Publications: Annual report.

*Community foundation incorporated in 1972 in Kentucky.

Contact: Linda L. Ball, Executive Director
    Application information: application form required
    Initial approach: letter
    Copies of proposal: 1
    Board meeting dates: June

The Dayton Foundation
1895 Kettering Tower
Dayton, Ohio 45423
(513) 222-0410

Restrictions: Grants for seed money, building funds, equipment, matching funds, technical assistance, internships, and special projects.

Focus of giving: Giving limited to Dayton and Montgomery County, Ohio.

$ Given: $337,965 for 76 grants: high $30,000; low $200; average $4,000–$5,000.

Publications: Annual report, application guidelines, and program policy statement.

Contact: Frederick Bartenstein, III, Director
    Initial approach: full proposal, telephone, or letter
    Copies of proposal: 1
    Deadlines: submit proposal preferably 2 weeks before board meeting
    Board meeting dates: bimonthly, beginning in January
    Final notification: 4 to 6 weeks

George H. Deuble Foundation*
P.O. Box 2288
North Canton, Ohio 44720
(216) 494-0494

Restrictions: Money for continuing support, annual campaigns, emergency funds, building funds, equipment, endowment funds, matching funds, conferences, and seminars.

Focus of giving: Giving primarily in the Stark County, Ohio area.

$ Given: $318,459 for grants: average $5,000.

Contact: Andrew H. Deuble, Trustee
   Initial approach: letter
   Deadlines: none
   Board meeting dates: monthly
   Final notification: 1 month

The George Gund Foundation**
One Erieview Plaza
Cleveland, Ohio 44114
(216) 241-3114

Restrictions: Grants for operating budgets, continuing support, annual campaigns, seed money, emergency funds, land acquisition, matching funds, internships, special projects, publications, conferences, and seminars.

*Trust established in 1947 in Ohio.

**Incorporated in 1951 in Ohio.

Focus of giving: Giving primarily in northeastern Ohio.

$ Given: $5,469,723 for 360 grants: high $500,000; low $600; average $22,000.

Publications: Annual report, program policy statement, and application guidelines.

Contact: Donald Bergholz, Executive Director
   Initial approach: full proposal
   Copies of proposal: 1
   Deadlines: January 15, April 15, August 15, and October 15
   Board meeting dates: March, June, October, and December
   Final notification: 8 weeks

The Nord Family Foundation*
6125 South Broadway
Elyria, Ohio 44053
(216) 324-2822

Restrictions: Grants for operating budgets, continuing support, annual campaigns, seed money, emergency funds, building funds, equipment, land acquisition, endowment funds, matching funds, consulting services, technical assistance, special projects, and publications.

Focus of giving: Giving limited to Lorain and Cuyahoga counties, Ohio and Atlanta, Georgia.

$ Given: $548,616 for 111 grants: high $40,000; low $25; average $2,000–$5,000. Also $105,000 for one loan.

---

*Trust established in 1952 in Ohio.

Publications: Annual report, program policy statement, and application guidelines.

Contact: Jeptha J. Carrell, Executive Director
> **Initial approach:** full proposal, letter, or telephone
> **Copies of proposal:** 1
> **Deadlines:** submit proposal at least six weeks before meetings; no set deadline
> **Board meeting dates:** January, June, and October
> **Final notification:** 1 to 3 months

The Stark County Foundation
1180 United Bank Building
220 Market Avenue South
Canton, Ohio 44702
(216) 454-3426

Restrictions: Grants for seed money, emergency funds, building funds, equipment, land acquisition, matching funds, special projects, research, conferences and seminars, consulting services, and technical assistance.

Focus of giving: Giving limited to Stark County, Ohio.

$ Given: $613,000 for 48 grants: high $100,000; low $200; average $5,000–$25,000. Also $53,000 for 61 loans.

Publications: Annual report, program policy statement, and application guidelines.

Contact: James A. Bower, Executive Secretary
> **Initial approach:** letter or full proposal
> **Copies of proposal:** 8
> **Deadlines:** none

Board meeting dates: monthly

Final notification: 60 to 90 days

OREGON

The Oregon Community Foundation
1110 Yeon Building
522 S.W. Fifth Avenue
Portland, Oregon 97204
(503) 227-6846

Restrictions: Grants for operating budgets, continuing support, seed money, building funds, equipment, land acquisition, endowment funds, technical assistance, and special projects.

Focus of giving: Giving limited to Oregon.

$ Given: $1,614,677 for 175 grants: high $50,000; low $500; average $2,500–$50,000.

Publications: Annual report, newsletter, program policy statement, and application guidelines.

Contact: Greg Chaille, Executive Director

    Application information: application form required

    Initial approach: letter

    Copies of proposal: 12

    Deadlines: submit application preferably in March or August; deadlines April 1 and September 1

    Board meeting dates: January, June, September, and November

    Final notification: 3 months

PENNSYLVANIA

The Philadelphia Foundation
Two Mellon Bank Center, Suite 2017
Philadelphia, Pennsylvania 19102
(215) 563-6417

Restrictions: Grants for operating budgets, continuing support, seed money, emergency funds, equipment, matching funds, special projects, consulting services, and technical assistance.

Focus of giving: Giving limited to Philadelphia, to Bucks and Chester counties in Delaware, and to Montgomery County in southeastern Pennsylvania, except for designated funds.

$ Given: $3,265,542 for 370 grants: high $81,601; low $183; average $500–$15,000.

Publications: Annual report, application guidelines, and program policy statement.

Contact: John E. Ruthrauff, Director
  Initial approach: full proposal
  Copies of proposal: 1
  Deadlines: submit proposal preferably during May and June or November and December; deadlines July 31 and January 15
  Board meeting dates: April and November
  Final notification: 3 to 4 months

Pittsburgh National Foundation
Fifth Avenue and Wood Street
Pittsburgh, Pennsylvania 15222
(412) 355-0904

Restrictions: Grants for operating budgets, continuing support, annual campaigns, seed money, emergency funds, deficit financing, general purposes, building funds, equipment, land acquisition, endowment funds, matching funds, employee matching gifts, technical assistance, program-related investments, research, special projects, publications, conferences, and seminars.

Focus of giving: Giving limited to southwestern Pennsylvania.

$ Given: $758,734 for 188 grants: high $240,000; low $75; average $250–$75,000. Also $19,900 for employee matching gifts.

Contact: Robert C. Milsom, Chairman, Pittsburgh National Bank (for written requests); William Boyd, Jr. (telephone contact)

   Initial approach: full proposal

   Copies of proposal: 1

   Deadlines: none

   Board meeting dates: monthly

   Final notification: 6 weeks

RHODE ISLAND

The Rhode Island Foundation*
957 North Main Street
Providence, Rhode Island 02904
(401) 274-4564

Restrictions: Grants for operating budgets, seed money, emergency funds, building funds, equipment, land acquisition, matching funds, consulting services, technical assistance, special projects, research, publications, conferences, and seminars.

Focus of giving: Giving limited to Rhode Island.

$ Given: $2,609,502 for 200 grants: high $125,000; low $500.

Publications: Annual report, program policy statement, and application guidelines.

Contact: Douglas M. Jansson, Executive Director
   Application information: priority given to first 25 applications received prior to each board meeting
   Initial approach: telephone, meeting, letter, or full proposal
   Copies of proposal: 8
   Board meeting dates: January, March, May, July, September, and November
   Final notification: 3 months

*Community foundation incorporated in 1916 in Rhode Island.

SOUTH CAROLINA

Foundation for the Carolinas
301 South Brevard Street
Charlotte, North Carolina
(704) 376-9541

Restrictions: Grants for operating budgets, seed money, emergency funds, building funds, equipment, matching funds, consulting services, technical assistance, land acquisition, special projects, and research.

Focus of giving: Giving primarily in North Carolina and South Carolina.

$ Given: $2,385,853 for 1,225 grants: high $209,800; low $100; average $500–$10,000. Also $12,398 for 15 grants to individuals and $4,000 for four loans.

Publications: Annual report, application guidelines, informational brochure, and newsletter.

Contact: William Spencer, President
    Application information: application form required
    Initial approach: letter
    Copies of proposal: 11
    Deadlines: none
    Board meeting dates: quarterly, with annual meeting in March; distribution committee meets monthly
    Final notification: 1 to 2 months

TEXAS

The El Paso Community Foundation*
Texas Commerce Bank Building, Suite 1616
El Paso, Texas 79901
(915) 533-4020

Restrictions: Grants for operating budgets, continuing support, annual campaigns, seed money, emergency funds, building funds, land acquisition, endowment funds, matching funds, special projects, publications, conferences, and seminars.

Focus of giving: Giving limited to the El Paso, Texas area.

$ Given: $505,542 for 155 grants.

Publications: Annual report and application guidelines.

Contact: Janice Windle, Executive Director

The Luling Foundation*
523 South Mulberry Avenue
P.O. Drawer 31
Luling, Texas 78648
(512) 875-2438

Restrictions: Local giving to help the farmer through demonstrations of farming techniques and to help the 4-H and FFA students of Caldwell, Gonzales, and Guadelupe counties for a period of two years with mar-

*Community foundation incorporated in 1977 in Texas
**Trust established in 1927 in Texas

keting show animals; principal activity is the operation of an agricultural demonstration farm. Money for special projects.

Focus of giving: Giving limited to Caldwell, Gonzales, and Guadalupe counties, Texas.

$ Given: $9,470 for seven grants: high $3,150; low $20; average $1,000. Also $3,000 for three grants to individuals, $43,858 for 18 foundation-administered programs, and $21,065 for 57 loans.

Publications: 990-PF, application guidelines, and information brochure.

Contact: Archie Abrameit, Manager

> **Application information:** application form required
>
> **Deadline:** April 30
>
> **Board meeting dates:** January, April, July, October, and as required

The Moody Foundation
704 Moody National Bank Building
Galveston, Texas 77550
(409) 763-5333

Restrictions: Funds to be used locally for historic restoration projects, performing arts organizations, cultural programs; for promotion of health, science, and education; for community and social services; and in the field of religion. Support given for seed money, emergency funds, building funds, equipment, consulting services, technical assistance, matching funds, special projects, research, publications, conferences, and seminars.

Focus of giving: Giving limited to Texas.

$ Given: $9,452,399 for 142 grants: high $515,000; low $600. Also $350,495 for 518 grants to individuals and $3,887,000 for three foundation-administered programs.

Publications: Annual report and application guidelines.

Contact: Peter M. Moore, Grants Officer
> **Initial approach:** letter or telephone
> **Copies of proposal:** 1
> **Deadlines:** 4 weeks prior to board meetings
> **Board meeting dates:** quarterly
> **Final notification:** 2 weeks after board meetings

WASHINGTON

Inland Northwest Community Foundation
400 Paulsen Center
Spokane, Washington 99201
(509) 624-2606

Restriction: Grants for operating budgets, continuing support, annual campaigns, equipment, land acquisition, endowment funds, matching funds, special projects, publications, seed money, building funds, consulting services, and technical assistance.

Focus of giving: Giving limited to the inland Northwest.

$ Given: $169,024 for 157 grants: high $3,500; low $242; average $1,000. Also $18,550 for 53 grants to individuals and $50 for employee matching gifts.

Publications: Annual report, program policy statement, application guidelines, and 990-PF.

Contact: Jeanne L. Ager, Executive Director
　　Application information: application form required
　　Initial approach: letter
　　Copies of proposal: 11
　　Deadlines: varies depending on area of grant
　　Board meeting dates: September through June
　　Final notification: 3 months

WEST VIRGINIA

Greater Ashland Foundation, Inc.*
1212 Bath Avenue
P.O. Box 2096
Ashland, Kentucky 41105
(606) 324-3888

Restrictions: Support for operating budgets, continuing support, seed money, emergency funds, consulting services, and technical assistance.

Focus of giving: Giving limited to the tristate area of Ashland, Kentucky; Ironton, Ohio; and Huntington, West Virginia.

$ Given: Expenditures: $291,741.

Publications: Annual report.

Contact: Linda L. Ball, Executive Director

*Community foundation incorporated in 1972 in Kentucky.

Application information: application form required

Initial approach: letter

Copies of proposal: 1

Board meeting date: June

The Greater Kanawha Valley Foundation*
P.O. Box 3041
Charleston, West Virginia
(304) 346-3620

Restrictions: Grants for operating budgets, continuing support, seed money, emergency funds, building funds, equipment, land acquisition, special projects, research, publications, conferences and seminars, consulting services, and technical assistance.

Focus of giving: Giving limited to the Greater Kanawha Valley, West Virginia area, except scholarships, which are limited to residents of West Virginia.

$ Given: $406,559 for 91 grants: high $25,000; low $89; average $500–$5,000. Also $200,371 for 200 grants to individuals.

Publications: Annual report and application guidelines.

Contact: Stanley Loewenstein, Executive Director

   Initial approach: full proposal

*Community foundation established in 1962 in West Virginia.

Copies of proposal: 1

Deadlines: 1st of April, July, October, and December

Board meeting dates: usually in April, July, October, and December

Final notification: immediately after board action

4

Flow-Through Funding by Area of Business

ECOLOGY

Whitehall Foundation, Inc.
249 Royal Palm Way, Suite 220
Palm Beach, Florida 33480
(407) 655-4474

Restrictions: Support for scholarly research in the life sciences, with emphasis on (1) plant physiology, development, genetics, and ecology, (2) ecology and population biology, (3) invertebrate neurophysiology; (4) animal behavior and ethology, and (5) taxonomy and phylogeny; innovative and imaginative projects preferred. Grants for seed money, equipment, technical assistance, special projects, research, and publications; grants also to individuals.

$ Given: $1,749,374 for 61 grants: high $80,000; low $3,450; average $25,000–$38,000.

Publications: 990-PF, program policy statement, and application guidelines.

Contact: Laurel T. Baker, Secretary

Application information: application form required

Initial approach: preliminary letter

Copies of proposal: 1

Deadlines: March 1, September 1, and December 1

Board meeting dates: November, but votes by mail in March, June, and December

Final notification: 5 to 9 months

ENVIRONMENT

Alaska Conservation Foundation*
430 West Seventh, Suite 215
Anchorage, Alaska 99501
(907) 276-1917

Restrictions: Research and education projects for environmental protection in Alaska. Grants for general purposes, continuing support, seed money, emergency funds, equipment, matching funds, consulting services, technical assistance, internships, research, special projects, conferences, seminars, and publications.

Focus of giving: Giving limited to Alaska. No grants for annual campaigns, deficit financing, building funds, land acquisition, renovation projects, general or special endowments, or program-related investments.

$ Given: $178,246 for 50 grants.

Publications: Annual report, program policy statement, and application guidelines.

*Community foundation incorporated in 1980 in Alaska.

Contact: Jim Stratton, Vice President

   Application information: application form required

The Arca Foundation
1425 21st Street, N.W.
Washington, D.C. 20036
(202) 822-9193

Restrictions: To promote the well-being of mankind
through grants to organizations primarily concerned
with U.S. foreign policy applications in Central America, toxicity and hazardous wastes, issues of a safe and
a healthy environment, community development, and
antipoverty programs. Programs should emphasize network building and decentralization. Grants for operating budgets, continuing support, seed money, technical assistance, publications, conferences, seminars, and
special projects.

$ Given: $643,850 for 47 grants: high $100,000; low
$500; average $13,700.

Publications: Annual report, application guidelines,
and program policy statement.

Contact: Janet Shenk, Executive Director

   Initial approach: letter

   Copies of proposal: 3

   Deadlines: submit summary of proposal preferably
   in January, February, July, or August; deadlines
   March 15 and September 15

   Board meeting dates: May and November

   Final notification: up to 6 months

GENETICS

Whitehall Foundation, Inc.
249 Royal Palm Way, Suite 220
Palm Beach, Florida 33480
(407) 655-4474

Restrictions: Support for scholarly research in the life sciences, with emphasis on (1) plant physiology, development, genetics, and ecology, (2) ecology and population biology, (3) invertebrate neurophysiology, (4) animal behavior and ethology, and (5) taxonomy and phylogeny; innovative and imaginative projects preferred. Grants for seed money, equipment, technical assistance, special projects, research, and publications; grants also to individuals.

$ Given: $1,749,374 for 61 grants: high $80,000; low $3,450; average $25,000–$38,000.

Publications: 990-PF, program policy statement, and application guidelines.

Contact: Laurel T. Baker, Secretary

    Application information: application form required

    Initial approach: preliminary letter

    Copies of proposal: 1

    Deadlines: March 1, September 1, and December 1

    Board meeting dates: November, but votes by mail in March, June, and December

    Final notification: 5 to 9 months

The Arca Foundation
1425 21st Street, N.W.
Washington, D.C. 20036
(202) 822-9193

Restrictions: To promote the well-being of mankind through grants to organizations primarily concerned with U.S. foreign policy applications in Central America, toxicity and hazardous wastes, issues of a safe and a healthy environment, community development, and antipoverty programs. Programs should emphasize network building and decentralization. Grants for operating budgets, continuing support, seed money, technical assistance, publications, conferences, seminars, and special projects.

$ Given: $643,850 for 47 grants: high $100,000; low $500; average $13,700.

Publications: Annual report, application guidelines, and program policy statement.

Contact: Janet Shenk, Executive Director
    Initial approach: letter
    Copies of proposal: 3
    Deadlines: submit summary of proposal preferably in January, February, July, or August; deadlines March 15 and September 15
    Board meeting dates: May and November
    Final notification: up to 6 months

JEWISH IMMIGRATION

The Baron de Hirsch Fund*
130 East 59th Street
New York, New York 10022
(212) 980-1000 ext. 1798

Restrictions: To assist in the economic assimilation of Jewish immigrants in the United States and Israel, their instruction in trades and agriculture, and promotion of agriculture among them; also aids other agencies that work to obtain education and jobs for immigrants. Grants for operating budgets, continuing support, seed money, emergency funds, exchange programs, special projects, research, conferences, and seminars; grants also to individuals.

$ Given: $311,000 for 14 grants: high $36,500; low $10,000; average $21,000. Also $42,925 for 37 grants to individuals.

Publications: Application guidelines.

Contact: Lauren Katzowitz, Managing Director
    Initial approach: letter
    Copies of proposal: 1
    Deadlines: submit proposal preferably between May and August; deadline September 1
    Board meeting date: October
    Final notification: 2 weeks after board meeting

*Incorporated in 1891 in New York.

RUSSIAN IMMIGRATION

The Trustees of Ivan V. Koulaieff Educational Fund*
c/o Nathan B. Siegel
3406 Geary Boulevard
San Francisco, California 94118

Restrictions: Aid to Russian immigrants throughout the world through grants, scholarships, and loans; support also for Russian Orthodox education and churches in the United States.

$ Given: $44,140 for 35 grants: high $2,450; low $180; Also $57,730 for 62 grants to individuals.

*Incorporated in 1930 in California.

FEDERAL MONEY

The grants in this section consist primarily of awards made by government agencies. In addition to these sources you may want to check with your local bank or Small Business Administration (SBA) office about the possibility of obtaining an SBA loan. The money is not cheap; as of the writing of this book, the interest rate is 2.25 percent above the prime rate. To meet the requirements of an SBA loan, you must have been turned down by a commercial lender and you must be able to collaterize the loan. The good news is that repayment note terms vary from 7 to 25 years; as SBA tries to keep their default rate at a minimum, they will structure the loan and work with the recipient to try to guarantee repayment. Most businesses are eligible for SBA assistance with a few exceptions, such as publishing, gambling, investment, or speculation in real estate.

Under the Small Business Investment Act, SBA licenses, regulates, and helps to provide financing of privately and publicly owned small business investment companies (SBICs). SBIC financing provides both start-up and expansion capital either in the form of a loan or for an equity position in the company.

Most buyers of this book will apply to receive financing from an SBIC, such as ITT in California. However, for those businesses that have some cash on hand—1 million dollars minimum—*creating* an SBIC offers an interesting and lucrative possibility. For example, motion picture company XYZ would benefit as follows:

1. The creation of the SBIC would save the XYZ Production Company 3 million dollars each year in their print and media costs alone.

2. The SBIC acts as a tax shelter for profits.

3. The SBIC would bring in additional revenues for XYZ Production Company aside from its film revenues, thus assuring profitability for XYZ Production Company. The creation of the SBIC will enable the XYZ Production Company to become a diversified corporation for a minimal investment.

4. The SBIC can serve the XYZ Production Company's own interests. The SBIC, for example, can be used to acquire up to a 40 percent interest in companies that serve the needs of XYZ Production Company. The SBIC could choose, for example, to invest in an ad agency, a media buying service—existing or start-up businesses that have tremendous potential for growth and that directly relate to the motion picture industry. For example, the XYZ Production Company would invest in a media placement service. XYZ Production Company would receive 40 percent of the profits of that service. As XYZ Production Company would assure 50 million dollars in billings per year, the agency would be guaranteed 7.5 million dollars in fees based on the standard 15 percent commission structure on the XYZ account alone. XYZ Production Company would receive 40 percent of earnings of said 7.5 million dollars or approximately 3 million dollars per year (less reasonable operating costs).

AGRICULTURE

AGRICULTURAL CONSERVATION PROGRAM

Agricultural Stabilization and Conservation Service
Department of Agriculture
P.O. Box 2415
Washington, D.C. 20013
(202) 447-7333

Restrictions: Control of erosion and sedimentation, voluntary compliance with federal and state requirements to solve point and nonpoint source pollution, priorities in the National Environmental Policy Act, improvement of water quality, and assurance of a continued supply of necessary food and fiber. The program is directed toward the solution of critical soil, water, woodland, and pollution abatement problems on farms and ranches. The conservation practices are to be used on agricultural land and must be performed satisfactorily and in accordance with applicable specifications.

$ Given: Direct payments of $3,800 a year, up to $10,000 with a pooling agreement; usually made for projects lasting a year, but the possibility exists of obtaining a three- to five-year agreement.

Contact: Conservation and Environmental Protection Division, ASCS

CONSERVATION RESERVE PROGRAM

Agricultural Stabilization and Conservation Service
(ASCS)
Department of Agriculture
P.O. Box 2415
Washington, D.C. 20013
(202) 447-7333

Restrictions: To protect the nation's long-term capability to produce food and fiber; reduce soil erosion, reduce sedimentation, improve water quality; create a better habitat for fish and wildlife, curb production of surplus commodities, and provide some needed income support for farmers.

Eligibility: Owners of private croplands who are willing to place highly erodible land under a ten-year contract. The participants, in return for annual payments, agree to implement a conservation plan developed by the local conservation district for converting highly erodible cropland to a less intensive use.

$ Given: Range and average of financial assistance: $50–$50,000.

Contact: Local or state ASCS office

COTTON PRODUCTION STABILIZATION (COTTON DIRECT PAYMENTS)

Agricultural Stabilization and Conservation Service (ASCS)
Department of Agriculture
P.O. Box 2415
Washington, D.C. 20013
(202) 447-7954

Restrictions: To attract the cotton production that is needed to meet domestic and foreign demand for fiber, to protect income for farmers, and to assure adequate supplies at fair and reasonable prices. Payments are used to provide producers with a guaranteed price whenever average prices drop below the established or "target" price.

Eligibility: Owner, landlord, tenant, or sharecropper on a farm where the commodity is planted that meets program requirements as announced by the Secretary of Agriculture.

$ Given: Direct payments ranging from $3 to $50,000.

Contact: Analysis Division, ASCS

CROP INSURANCE

**Crop Insurance
Manager
Federal Crop Insurance Corporation
Department of Agriculture
Washington, D.C. 20250
(202) 447-6795**

Restrictions: To improve agricultural stability through a sound system of crop insurance by providing all-risk insurance for individual farmers that will assure a basic income against droughts, freezes, insects, and other natural causes of disastrous crop losses. Insurance is available on crops in over 1,500 agricultural counties in 29 states.

$ Given: Insurance ranging from $1 to $250,000.

EMERGENCY CONSERVATION PROGRAM

**Conservation and Environmental Protection Division
Agricultural Stabilization and Conservation Service
Department of Agriculture
P.O. Box 2415
Washington, D.C. 20013
(202) 447-6221**

Restrictions: To enable farmers to perform emergency conservation measures to control wind erosion on farmlands—or to rehabilitate farmlands damaged by wind erosion, floods, hurricanes, or other natural disasters—and to carry out emergency water conservation or water-enhancing measures during periods of severe drought.

$ Given: For total amount of damage, payments of 64 percent are made for the first $62,500, 40 percent for the next $62,500, and 20 percent for the next $62,500 worth of damage. Maximum payment limitation of $200,000 per person per disaster.

FISH POND STOCKING

Fish and Wildlife Service
Richard B. Russell Federal Building #13641
75 Spring Street S.W.
Atlanta, Georgia 30303
(404) 331-3576

Restrictions: To supply fish to stock new or reclaimed farm and ranch ponds in Tennessee and Mississippi.

Contact: John Brown, Assistant Regional Director

FEED GRAIN PRODUCTION STABILIZATION (FEED GRAIN DIRECT PAYMENTS)

Production Adjustment Division
Agricultural Stabilization and Conservation Service (ASCS)
Department of Agriculture
P.O. Box 2415
Washington, D.C. 20013
(202) 447-5422

Restrictions: To attract the production needed to meet domestic and foreign demand, to protect income for farmers and to assure adequate supplies at fair and reasonable prices. Payments are used to provide producers with a guaranteed price on their planted acreage in the event the average prices drop below the established or "target" price.

Eligibility: Owner, landlord, tenant, or sharecropper on a farm where the commodity is planted that meets program requirements as announced by the Secretary of Agriculture.

$ Given: Direct payments, based on number of bushels produced, to a maximum of $50,000.

Contact: State or county ASCS

FORESTRY INCENTIVES PROGRAM

Agricultural Stabilization and Conservation Service (ASCS)
Department of Agriculture
P.O. Box 2415
Washington, D.C. 20013
(202) 447-7334

Restrictions: To bring private nonindustrial forest land under intensified management, to increase timber production, to assure adequate supplies of timber, and to enhance other forest resources through a combination of public and private investment on the most productive sites on eligible individual or consolidated ownerships of efficient size and operation.

Eligibility: Individuals who own nonindustrial private forest lands capable of producing industrial wood crops are eligible for cost-sharing assistance.

$ Given: Cost sharing up to 65 percent is authorized. States may set a lower level.

Contact: Conservation and Environmental Protection Division, ASCS

GRAIN RESERVE PROGRAM
(FARMER HELD AND OWNED GRAIN RESERVE)

Agricultural Stabilization and Conservation Service (ASCS)
Department of Agriculture
P.O. Box 2415
Washington, D.C. 20013
(202) 382-9886

Restrictions: To insulate sufficient quantities of grain from the market to increase price to farmers, improve and stabilize farm income and to assist farmers in the orderly marketing of their crops.

$ Given: Direct payments ranging from $25 to $50,000.

Contact: Cotton, Grain, and Rice Price Support Division, ASCS

GREAT PLAINS CONSERVATION

Soil Conservation Service
Department of Agriculture
P.O. Box 2890
Washington, D.C. 20013
(202) 382-1870

Restrictions: To conserve and develop the Great Plains soil and water resources by providing technical and financial assistance to farmers, ranchers, and others in planning and implementing conservation practices. Funds are available only for soil and water conservation measures determined to be needed to protect and stabilize a farm or ranch unit against climatic and erosion hazards.

$ Given: Direct payments up to $35,000.

Contact: Program Manager for Great Plains

NATIONAL WOOL ACT PAYMENTS
(WOOL AND MOHAIR)

Emergency Operations and Livestock Programs Division
Department of Agriculture
P.O. Box 2415
Washington, D.C. 20013
(202) 447-7673

Restrictions: To encourage increased domestic production of wool at prices fair to both producers and consumers in a way that has the least effect on domestic and foreign trade and to encourage producers to improve the quality and marketing of their wool and mohair.

Eligibility: Any person who owns sheep or lambs for 30 days or more and sells shorn wool or unshorn lambs during the marketing year. Any person who owns angora goats for 30 days or more and sells mohair produced therefrom.

$ Given: Direct payments to bring shorn wool to $1.80 a pound and to bring mohair to $4.93 a pound. Changes yearly.

Contact: Local Agricultural Stabilization and Conservation Service office

VERY-LOW-INCOME-HOUSING REPAIR LOANS AND GRANTS

Administrator, Farmers Home Administration
Department of Agriculture
14th Street and Independence Avenue, S.W.
Washington, D.C. 20250
(202) 447-4323

Restrictions: To give very-low-income rural homeowners an opportunity to make essential repairs to their homes—to make them safe and to remove health hazards to the family or the community. This includes repairs to the foundation, roof, or basic structure, as well as water and waste disposal systems and weatherization.

$ Given: Grants ranging from $400 to $5,000 over homeowner's lifetime (Section 504 loans and/or grants are for very-low-income homeowners; Section 502 loans are for the purchase, construction, or repair of low-income housing).

WHEAT DEFICIENCY PAYMENTS

Agricultural Stabilization and Conservation Service (ASCS)
Department of Agriculture
P.O. Box 2415
Washington, D.C. 20013
(202) 447-4146

Restrictions: To attract the production that is needed to meet domestic and foreign demand for food, to protect income for farmers, and to assure adequate supplies at fair and reasonable prices. Payments are used to provide producers with a guaranteed price on their planted acreage in the event average prices drop below the established or "target" price.

$ Given: Deficiency payments are established for each crop year in order to bring the price of wheat up to the national target rate.

Contact: Analysis Division, ASCS

WHEAT PRODUCTION STABILITY

Agricultural Stabilization and Conservation Service (ASCS)
Department of Agriculture
P.O. Box 2415
Washington, D.C. 20013
(202) 447-4146

Restrictions: To assure adequate production for domestic and foreign demand, to protect income for farmers, and to assure adequate supplies at fair and reasonable prices.

Eligibility: Owner, landlord, tenant, or sharecropper on a farm where the commodity is planted that meets program requirements as announced by the Secretary of Agriculture.

$ Given: $3,018 average deficiency payment per producer and $1,322 average diversion payment per producer.

Contact: ASCS county office

AIRLINES

Office of Aviation Analysis
Department of Transportation
400 Seventh Street, S.W., Room 5100
Washington, D.C. 20590
(202) 366-5903

Restrictions: To provide essential air transportation to eligible communities by subsidizing air service. Payments are made to air carriers to provide essential air services that could not be provided without a subsidy.

$ Given: Direct payments (negotiated with carriers who submit bids).

BUSINESS: EMPLOYMENT

Employment and Training Administration
Department of Labor
200 Constitution Avenue, N.W.
Washington, D.C. 20210
(202) 635-0672

Restrictions: To support employment and training studies that develop policy and programs for achieving the fullest utilization of the nation's human resources, to improve and strengthen the functioning of the nation's employment and training system, to develop new approaches to facilitate employment of the difficult to employ, and to conduct research and development addressing the employment implications of long-term social and economic trends and forces.

$ Given: Grants ranging from $1,000 to $1,000,000.

Contact: Director, Office of Research and Development

BUSINESS: INVENTORS

NBS Office of Energy-Related Inventions
National Institute of Standards and Technology
Building 202, Room 209
Gaithersburg, Maryland 20899
(301) 975-5500

Restrictions: To encourage innovation in developing non-nuclear energy technology by providing assistance to individual inventors and small business research and development companies in the development of promising energy-related inventions.

$ Given: Use of property, facilities, and equipment; also grants averaging $70,000.

CONSERVATION

GREAT PLAINS CONSERVATION

Soil Conservation Service
Department of Agriculture
P.O. Box 2890
Washington, D.C. 20013
(202) 447-4525

Restrictions: To conserve and develop the Great Plains soil and water resources by providing technical and financial assistance to farmers, ranchers, and others in planning and implementing conservation practices. Funds area available only for soil and water conservation measures determined to be needed to protect and stabilize a farm or ranch unit against climatic and erosion hazards.

$ Given: Direct payments up to $35,000.

WATER BANK PROGRAM

Agricultural Stabilization and Conservation Service (ASCS)
Department of Agriculture
P.O. Box 2415
Washington, D.C. 20013
(202) 447-4053

Restrictions: To conserve surface waters, preserve and improve migratory waterfowl habitat and wildlife resources, and secure other environmental benefits. Agreements are for 10 years with eligible landowners to help preserve important breeding and nesting areas of migratory waterfowl. In return for annual payments, the participants agree not to drain, burn, fill, or otherwise destroy the wetland character of such areas and not to use areas for agricultural purposes.

$ Given: Direct payments ranging from $7 to $66 per acre.

Contact: Conservation and Environmental Protection Division, ASCS

CONSTRUCTION: MASS TRANSIT

Urban Mass Transportation Administration
Office of Transit Assistance
400 Seventh Street, S.W.
Washington, D.C. 20590
(202) 366-1609

Restrictions: To assist in financing the acquisition, construction, reconstruction, and improvement of facilities and equipment for use (by operation, lease, or otherwise) in mass transportation service in urban areas and to assist in coordinating service with highway and other transportation in such areas.

$ Given: Grants ranging from $20,000 to $100,000,000.

Contact: Office of Grants Assistance

CONSTRUCTION: MINORITIES

Minority Contractors Assistance Project (MCAP)
89-50 164th Street, Suite 2B
Jamaica, New York 11432
(718) 657-6444

Restrictions: Provides bonding, financial, technical, and management assistance to minority and small construction contractors in cities for the purpose of "assisting the contractors to compete for a more equitable share of the construction industry." Services include: surety bonding program; financial and construction management; financial analysis; construction project management, including estimating, engineering, joint venture, and consortia arrangements; and procurement referrals for several federally funded building programs. Sponsors conferences and workshops on matters of particular interest to minority contractors, such as bonding and nonprofit housing. Operates MCAP Bonding and Insurance Agency, a for-profit subsidiary.

CONSTRUCTION: SHIPPING

Maritime Administration
Department of Transportation
400 Seventh Street, S.W.
Washington, D.C. 20590
(202) 426-4000

Restrictions: To promote the construction, reconstruction, reconditioning, or acquisition of merchant vessels necessary for national defense and the development of U.S. commerce.

$ Given: Direct payments (dollar amount not available).

Contact: Shipping Finance Office

Maritime Administration
Department of Transportation
400 Seventh Street, S.W.
Washington, D.C. 20590
(202) 426-4000

Restrictions: To provide for replacement vessels, additional vessels, or reconstructed vessels, built and documented under the laws of the United States for operation in the United States' foreign, Great Lakes, or noncontiguous domestic trades.

$ Given: Direct payments in the form of tax benefits.

Contact: Shipping Finance Office

**Maritime Administration
Department of Transportation
400 Seventh Street, S.W.
Washington, D.C. 20590
(202) 426-4000**

Restrictions: To promote the development and maintenance of the U.S. Merchant Marine by granting financial
aid to equalize cost of construction of a new ship in a
U.S. shipyard with the cost of constructing the same ship
in a foreign shipyard.

$ Given: Direct payments averaging $3,182,000.

Contact: Shipping Finance Office

CONSTRUCTION: TRANSPORTATION

**Office of Technology Development and Deployment
Urban Mass Transportation Administration
Department of Transportation
400 Seventh Street, S.W.
Washington, D.C. 20590
(202) 366-4020**

Restrictions: To improve the efficiency, effectiveness,
and productivity of transit services and equipment.

$ Given: Grants (dollar amount not available).

ENGINEERING

National Institute of General Medical Sciences
National Institute of Health
533 Westbard Avenue, DRG-Room 449
Bethesda, Maryland 20205
(301) 496-7463

Restrictions: To support the basic research that applies concepts from mathematics, physics, and engineering to biological systems, that uses engineering principles in the development of computers for patient monitoring, or that is related to physiology, anesthesiology, trauma and burn studies, and related areas.

$ Given: Grants ranging from $16,380 to $979,633.

Contact: Director, Physiology and Biomedical Engineering

HEALTH INSURANCE/SERVICES

National Center for Health Services Research
Public Health Service
Department of Health and Human Services
Parklawn Building, Room 18A20
5600 Fishers Lane
Rockville, Maryland 20857
(301) 443-4033

Restrictions: To support research, development, demonstration, and evaluation activities aimed toward developing new options for health services delivery and health policy; to test the assumptions on which current policies and delivery practices are based; and to develop the means for monitoring the performance of the health care system. Also to support research for the development of useful information to communities that are implementing Emergency Medical Services Systems (EMS). The program supports studies in many categories of concern, including cost containment, health insurance, planning and regulation, technology, and computer science applications.

$ Given: Grants ranging from $20,000 and up.

IMPORT/EXPORT: INDIVIDUALS

Employment and Training Administration
Department of Labor
601 D Street, N.W., Room 6434
Washington, D.C. 20213
(202) 376-6896

Restrictions: To provide adjustment assistance to workers adversely affected by increase of imports of articles similar to or directly competitive with articles produced by such workers' firms.

$ Given: Specialized services and direct weekly payments.

Contact: Director, Office of Trade Adjustment Assistance

MINORITIES

Interracial Council for Business Opportunity
800 Second Avenue, Suite 1309
New York, New York 10017
(212) 599-0677

Restrictions: To assist minority businessmen and businesswomen to develop, own, and manage business ventures with substantial employment and economic impact. Services include business feasibility studies, financing, market development, and other technical assistance to start or expand minority-owned companies. Offers free management training courses. Program operates nationally from New York City headquarters.

$ Given: Technical assistance.

Minority Business Development Agency (MBDA)
Department of Commerce
14th Street and Constitution Avenue, N.W.
Room 5073
Washington, D.C. 20230
(202) 377-1936

Restrictions: To provide money to businesses who are willing to provide free financial, management, and technical assistance to economically and socially disadvantaged individuals who need help in starting and/or operating a business. Primary objectives of the assistance are to increase the gross receipts and decrease the failure rates of the client firms.

$ Given: Grants ranging from $10,000 to $2,145,000, with the average award being around $213,000.

OCCUPATIONAL SAFETY

Occupational Safety and Health Administration (OSHA)
Department of Labor
200 Constitution Avenue, N.W.
Washington, D.C. 20210
(202) 523-9361

Restrictions: To assure safe and healthful working conditions.

$ Given: Dissemination of technical information and investigation of complaints.

Contact: Area office

Procurement and Grants Office
Centers for Disease Control
PHS/DHHS
255 East Paces Ferry Road
MSE 14
Atlanta, Georgia 30305
(404) 842-6575

Restrictions: To understand the underlying characteristics of occupational safety and health problems; to discover effective solutions in dealing with them; to eliminate or control factors in the work environment that are harmful to the health and safety of workers; and to demonstrate technical feasibility or application of new or improved occupational safety and health procedures, methods, techniques, or systems.

$ Given: Grants ranging from $5,000 to $150,000.

OVERSEAS INVESTMENTS

Investor Information
Overseas Private Investment Corporation
1616 M Street, N.W.
Washington, D.C. 20257
(202) 457-7200

Restrictions: Financing for overseas investment.

$ Given: Loans.

PUBLISHING

Assistant Director
Publication Subvention Program
National Endowment for the Humanities, Room 319
Washington, D.C. 20506
(202) 786-0204

Restrictions: To ensure, through grants to publishing entities, the dissemination of works of scholarly distinction that without support could not be published.

$ Given: Direct payments up to $35,000.

RANCHING: CONSERVATION

Soil Conservation Service
Department of Agriculture
P.O. Box 2890
Washington, D.C. 20013
(202) 382-1870

Restrictions: To conserve and develop the Great Plains soil and water resources by providing technical and financial assistance to farmers, ranchers, and others in planning and implementing conservation practices. Funds are available only for soil and water conservation measures determined to be needed to protect and stabilize a farm or ranch unit against climatic and erosion hazards.

$ Given: Direct payments up to $35,000.

Contact: Program Manager for Great Plains

REAL ESTATE

Office of Real Property
Federal Property Resource Service
General Services Administration
Washington, D.C. 20405
(202) 535-7084

Restrictions: To dispose of surplus real property. Surplus real property may be conveyed for public work or recreation use and public health or educational purposes at discounts up to 100 percent. It can also be used for public airport purposes, wildlife conservation, replacement housing, historic monument purposes without monetary consideration, and for general public purposes without restrictions at a price equal to the estimated fair market value of the property.

$ Given: Sale, exchange, or donation of property.

REAL ESTATE: PERSONAL PROPERTY

Office of Personal Property
Federal Property Resources Service
General Services Administration
Washington, D.C. 20405
(202) 535-7000

Restrictions: To sell property no longer needed by the government in an economical and efficient manner and obtain the maximum net return from sales. The General Services Administration conducts the sale of personal property for most of the civil agencies; the Department of Defense handles the sale of its own surplus property.

$ Given: Sale, exchange, or donation of property and goods.

Contact: Director, Sales Division

REAL ESTATE: RENTAL HOUSING FOR LOWER-INCOME FAMILIES

Department of Housing and Urban Development
Elderly and Handicapped Division
451 Seventh Street, S.W.
Washington, D.C. 20410
(202) 755-5216

Restrictions: To make good quality rental housing available to low-income families who are elderly and handicapped at a cost they can afford by making payments to owners of approved multifamily rental housing projects to supplement the partial rental payments of eligible tenants.

$ Given: Loans (dollar amount not available).

Contact: Director, Office of Multifamily Housing Management and Occupancy, Housing

SHIPPING

Maritime Administration
Department of Transportation
400 Seventh Street, S.W.
Washington, D.C. 20590
(202) 366-1905

Restrictions: To promote the development and maintenance of U.S. Merchant Marine by granting financial aid to equalize cost of operating a U.S. flagship with cost of operating a competitive foreign flagship.

$ Given: Direct payments ranging from $5,008 to $8,085 per day.

Contact: Assistant Administrator for Maritime Aids

Resource List

The following organizations provide program-related investment opportunities and/or consulting services.

Affirmative Investments
129 South Street, Sixth Floor
Boston, Massachusetts 02111
(617) 350-0250
Barbara Cleary, President

Provides advisor services to those who seek to achieve progressive social objectives through alternative investments.

Cooperative Assistance Fund
2100 M Street, N.W.
Suite 306
Washington, D.C. 20037
(202) 833-8543
Herman "Tex" Wilson, President

A pool of program-related investment funds used to finance minority and community-based enterprises.

The Enterprise Foundation
505 American City Building
Columbia, Maryland 21044
(301) 964-1230
Paul Brophy, President

Seeks alternative investments for housing finance (for the very poor).

Fund for an Open Society
311 South Juniper, Suite 400
Philadelphia, Pennsylvania
19107
(215) 735-6915

Nonprofit mortgage company that provides low-interest financing to encourage racially integrated housing, using PRIs and other socially motivated investments.

Housing Assistance
  Council
1025 Vermont Avenue,
  N.W.
Washington, D.C. 20005
(202) 842-8600

Harold O. Wilson, Executive
  Director

Assists rural community-
based organizations to raise
investments for low-income
housing projects.

Industrial Cooperative
  Association
249 Elm Street
Somerville, Massachusetts
  02144

Steven Dawson, Executive
  Director
Laura Henze, Director, ICA
  Revolving Loan Fund

This loan fund seeks grants
and investments to finance
worker-owned cooperatives.

Institute for Community
  Economics, Inc.
151 Montague City Road
Greenfield, Massachusetts
01301
(413) 774-7956

Charles Matthei, Director

Provides technical assistance
and loan funds to land trusts
and community groups working on housing and commu-
nity development strategies.

Local Initiatives Support
  Corporation (LISC)
666 Third Avenue
New York, New York 10017
(212) 949-8560

Paul Grogan, President

Organized by a coalition of
corporations and foundations,
LISC finances enterprises that
are sponsored by neighbor-
hood-based organizations.

National Cooperative Bank
  Development Corporation
1630 Connecticut Avenue,
N.W. Washington, D.C.
20009
(202) 745-4617

Thomas S. Condit,
  President

As the development arm of the
National Cooperative Bank,
the corporation assists projects appropriate for foundation PRIs, including worker-owned stores in inner-city
neighborhoods.

National Housing Law
  Project
1950 Addison Street
Berkeley, California 94704
(415) 948-9400
Dan Perlman

Assists community-based
organizations to raise investment funds for low-income
housing projects.

National Rural Development
  and Finance Corporation
1718 Connecticut Avenue,
  N.W.
Washington, D.C. 20009
(202) 466-6950
Neal Nathanson

Financial intermediary that
channels investments to economic development ventures
sponsored by community organizations in low-income rural
areas.

National Trust for
  Historic Preservation
1785 Massachusetts Ave.,
  N.W.
Washington, D.C. 20036
(202) 673-4000

Operates the Inner-City Ventures Fund, which channels
PRIs and other resources to
historic preservation projects
sponsored by low-income, community-based organizations.
Also operates revolving funds
for other historic preservation
projects.